THE ANALYSIS
OF SOCIAL CHANGE

THE ANALYSIS
OF SOCIAL CHANGE

BASED ON OBSERVATIONS
IN CENTRAL AFRICA

BY

GODFREY & MONICA WILSON

CAMBRIDGE
At the University Press
1968

PUBLISHED BY
THE SYNDICS OF THE CAMBRIDGE UNIVERSITY PRESS

Bentley House, 200 Euston Road, London, N.W. 1
American Branch: 32 East 57th Street, New York, N.Y. 10022

Standard Book Numbers:
521 06820 7 clothbound
521 09554 9 paperback

First published 1945
Reprinted   1954
             1965
First paperback
    edition 1968

First printed in Great Britain at the University Press, Cambridge
Reprinted in Great Britain by Hazell Watson & Viney Ltd,
Aylesbury, Bucks

CONTENTS

ACKNOWLEDGMENT

The bulk of the ideas in this book are current in sociological theory. Where we are particularly conscious of a debt we have made acknowledgment in a footnote, but the absence of such detailed reference does not imply a claim to originality. Our ideas have developed slowly, with reading and in discussion with colleagues, and we ourselves are often uncertain of their source. Dr Audrey Richards, Dr Meyer Fortes and Dr Max Gluckman have read and criticised the manuscript and to them we are especially grateful.

The field work in Central Africa on which the study is based was financed by the Rockefeller Foundation and the International Institute of African Languages and Cultures, to whom we are indebted for Fellowships, and by the Rhodes-Livingstone Institute of Northern Rhodesia.

G. W.

M. W.

NORTHERN RHODESIA
SOUTH AFRICA
MIDDLE EAST

CHAPTER I

CENTRAL AFRICAN SOCIETY: A PROBLEM FOR ANALYSIS

(a) INTRODUCTORY

IN trying to understand men's relations in Central Africa to-day we have assumed that a science of sociology is possible; that is, that there are necessary connections between social facts which can be discovered. Seeking these connections in Central Africa we have formulated a number of hypotheses. These, being scientific, are tentative; and the limitations of our own knowledge, which prevent our testing them out in a wide range of historical situations, make it all the more necessary for us to emphasize their tentative character. They do, however, seem to illuminate the particular field of Central Africa; and it is of this alone that we seek to persuade you. If we succeed in doing so it may then be worth considering their wider relevance; for connections established in one situation must, albeit qualified and reformulated, be applicable in others also.

We speak of 'Central Africa' in order to avoid cumbersome phrases, but our field is more limited than this term at first suggests. We exclude the old Arab civilization of the east coast, except in so far as through ivory and slave traders it affected the interior. We exclude also the non-British territories—the Belgian Congo, Portuguese East Africa and Angola—with which we have no acquaintance. The field to which we refer consists of Tanganyika, Nyasaland and Northern Rhodesia, with the exception of the coastal belt of Tanganyika.

Within this field we have a detailed knowledge of three

African groups—the Nyakyusa of south Tanganyika, with whom we lived for nearly three years (1934–8); the people of Ngonde (1937), which is a district in north Nyasaland, whose language and culture resembles that of the adjoining Nyakyusa; and the semi-detribalized urban group in Broken Hill, Northern Rhodesia (1939–40). We have also visited the Lupa gold fields in south Tanganyika (1937), on which the Nyakyusa and the people of Ngonde together provide a third of the African labour; and one of us has visited the Bemba tribe in north-eastern Rhodesia (1938), which provides another third of that labour. To the old social system of the Bemba we have constantly to refer, and in doing so we rely on the work of Audrey Richards who has studied them intensively (1930–4). The urban group in Broken Hill is largely drawn from the Bemba and allied tribes in north-eastern Rhodesia.

For material on other groups we rely on the work of Smith and Dale among the Ila of Northern Rhodesia, of Read among the Ngoni of Nyasaland and Northern Rhodesia, of Gluckman among the Lozi of Northern Rhodesia, of the Culwicks on the Bena of Tanganyika, and on Government reports. Some comparative evidence is drawn from the Union of South Africa, where one of us did field work in a reserve (Pondoland), in town locations, and on European farms (1931–3).

(b) From Primitive to Civilized

Within living memory men's relations in Central Africa were primitive; now they are being very rapidly civilized. Merely to chronicle this change, in however great detail, is not to understand it. A chronicle gives us little light on what has determined the changes which have taken place, and what their future implications are likely to be. We look therefore for the connections between the changes taking place, and in finding these seek to demonstrate what changes must follow, if certain others are made.

We observe, for instance, that in the primitive societies kinship had a very great importance; that in the more civilized groups of the modern world it has far less importance, and that among Africans the traditional importance of many relations of kinship is decreasing. Thus far it is mere chronicle. But, we ask, is this change in kinship a necessary concomitant of the change from primitive to civilized, or is it characteristic only of particular civilizations? Is a policy aimed at maintaining the traditional kinship obligations likely to be successful? Can a Government assume that under modern conditions Africans will continue to support infirm relatives? And so on.

(i) *Economic Changes*

The economy of the primitive societies was one of subsistence agriculture, or subsistence pastoralism, or a mixture of both, with the addition of a few simple crafts. There was little specialization, and, with one great exception, there was only local trade. Each village or settlement—and most of these were small—produced nearly everything it needed. The one great exception to this local self-sufficiency was the trade in ivory and slaves, which linked some, though not all, of the tribes of Central Africa to the outside world. Cloth, beads, and muzzle-loading guns flowed in; ivory and slaves flowed out; and this trade affected the structure even of remote tribes. Except along the main trade routes, however, the relations involved were tenuous, and local self-sufficiency remained the dominant feature of economic life. The only means of transport were man-power and dugout canoes, the use of which was limited by the absence, in many areas, of navigable water. There were no wheeled vehicles, and riding and pack animals were rarely used. Money was unknown.

There was little capital accumulation down the generations; for such capital equipment as existed was mostly as perishable as man, while skill and knowledge—which also have a capital value—had only the narrow channels of oral tradition and personal example in which to flow.

The economy of Central Africa to-day is part of a world organization; there is no longer any local self-sufficiency. Foreign cloth and foreign hoes have now become necessities of life for the majority of the African population, while foreign bicycles and sewing machines, tin dishes, ploughs, and padlocks are increasingly bought. Payment for these foreign goods is made by the export of copper, vanadium, zinc, lead, tobacco, beeswax and timber from Northern Rhodesia; sisal, gold, rice, tea and coffee from Tanganyika; cotton, tea and tobacco from Nyasaland. Even the most remote villages are intimately affected by fluctuations in the price of these on the world market.

With the foreign trade, an internal trade between the newly grown towns and the country has developed. The town workers buy goods from the peasants, and the peasants buy foreign goods in town. At the same time some old businesses have increased in range. Pots made on the shores of Lake Nyasa, for example, are sold over a much wider area than formerly, and dried fish reaches villages where none came before. Railways and metalled roads have been built, and lorries and bicycles have largely displaced the porter. The principal towns are linked by air services. Everywhere money is in general use.

Not only is Central Africa now a specialized unit in the world economy, importing some goods and exporting others, but internally also its economy is much more specialized than before. The raising of food is no longer everyone's business. Formerly the few specialized workers, such as smiths and doctors, engaged in subsistence farming like their neighbours, and practised their specializations only in their spare time. But to-day production for export, commerce, government, religion, education and transport engage a host of full-time workers whose food is supplied by others. The most obvious mark of this is the growth of towns. The number of different specialisms, moreover, has grown enormously.

In comparison with the more civilized areas of the modern world, however, the economy of Central Africa is still relatively unspecialized. Villages usually raise most of their own food, and build their own houses without outside help, and without dividing the processes among the different families. Nor has the multiplication of specialisms anywhere yet equalled that of more civilized lands. Specialization and interdependence with distant groups have grown continuously for fifty years, and seem still to be growing.

The capital accumulated by many centuries of civilization is being increasingly used in Central Africa. Millions of pounds worth of capital equipment has been imported in the form of mining plant, railway stock, improved livestock, commercial and farm equipment; while the accumulated knowledge and skills of civilization are being applied to the development of the country. The standard of living has risen considerably.

In sum, we have here a contrast between a number of unspecialized, locally self-sufficient, non-accumulating, and poor primitive economies, and a highly differentiated, universally interdependent, rapidly accumulating, and rich civilized economy. We observe that economic activity in Central Africa has steadily approximated in type to the second and seems to be still doing so. We seek the necessary implications of this economic change. How does it affect law and religion? Is it necessarily connected with the decline in the importance of kinship?

(ii) *Political Changes*

The political units of old Central Africa were small. Law was often effective in groups of a few thousand only. Occasional paramount chiefs were honoured by as many as four hundred thousand people, but even in their areas investigation often reveals an absence of political unity, the constituent chiefdoms recognizing no common legal authority, and war being endemic among them.[1] Political authority was closely linked with religious status and with personal wealth; chiefs, headmen, and elders being usually the high-priests of their respective areas, and the richest men in them.

To-day the three Territories each include scores of previously independent political units, and are themselves integral parts of the British Empire of 540,000,000 people. Peace is enforced and law is effective throughout the Empire and, by international agreement, beyond its boundaries. All three Territories are administered through the traditional authorities on the principle of 'indirect rule', but these authorities are under the control of British administrative officers stationed throughout the country, and each Territory has a Central Government. Policy is directed from London and is affected by political conditions in Europe. The form of local administration in Tanganyika, for example, was radically altered because Germany was defeated in 1918, and subsequent policy has been modified by the fact that Tanganyika is a Mandated Territory, not a Colony.

[1] Cf. Godfrey Wilson, *The Constitution of Ngonde*, Rhodes-Livingstone Papers, No. 3, 1939.

Within this large system local centralization is continuously going on. While some of the traditional authorities, such as paramount chiefs and their councils, are increasing in judicial and administrative power, others—village headmen, village elders, and many local chiefs—are losing this power. In some places new paramountcies or tribal councils have been created, where none but local authorities existed before.

Political authority in the new system is less immediately linked with religious status and wealth. Among the Europeans, Church and State are separately organized, different people having the highest status in each, while the wealthiest men are not always those in positions of great authority. Among the Africans a similar differentiation is becoming more and more evident. The religious power of the traditional authorities is being transferred to European missionaries and to African ministers and elders; in wealth they are no longer solely prominent, being equalled or outdone by their subjects who have become clerks and shopkeepers and mechanics.

We seek to discover how this change from a number of small, locally decentralized organizations, within which political authority was closely linked with religious and economic status, to an enormous, centralized organization, within which authority is less immediately linked with religious and economic status, is related to the economic changes already described. Is a high degree of centralization inevitable in a civilized society?

(iii) *Technical and Scientific Changes*

The language areas of old Central Africa were small. Mutual understanding was sometimes confined to a few thousand people, and nowhere, we think, exceeded half a million. Though the languages were nearly all related, it appears that a very small proportion of the population spoke any but their own.

To-day English is spoken by practically all the immigrants and by an increasing number of Africans. Of the Africans over 10 years of age in Nyasaland 6 % claim some knowledge of English.[1] Four or five African languages are dominating the others. Swahili is used in trade and administration, and is taught in schools, all over Tanganyika; it is not confined to the coast and slave routes, as formerly. Nyanja is spreading in Nyasaland; and Nyanja, Bemba and Kololo in Northern Rhodesia. A *lingua franca*, 'kitchen Kaffir', is considerably used, and affords a degree of understanding between European and African, and between Africans of different tribes. Communication is further facilitated by a decrease in dialect differences. The people of Ngonde and the neighbouring Nyakyusa, for instance, say that they could hardly understand one another in the old days, and the speech of the old men is still markedly different, but that of the young men is now almost identical.

As there was a certain similarity of grammar and vocabulary between the different Bantu languages of old Central Africa, so there was a general similarity in the crafts of the people who spoke them. It is easy to mistake a flat Ndali basket for one from Kalobo many hundred miles away, or a Bemba beer strainer from Northern Rhodesia for one from Pondoland on the South African coast. Nyakyusa and Pondo sleeping mats are hardly distinguishable to the untrained eye. But the details of style were as local as languages. The decoration and strands of the weave differ in Ndali and Kalobo baskets, as do the edges of Bemba and Pondo beer strainers. Museum experts can place spears and pots, baskets and bead skirts by peculiarities of construction and ornament. Most arte-

[1] *Nyasaland Protectorate, Census Report*, 1931.

facts had only a local circulation, and since lasting mediums were scarce, the artefacts passed down the generations were few. Excavations on Bantu sites yield little but skeletons, potsherds and occasional iron tools. All the old techniques were, by modern standards, very simple ones.

Now local differences in style of dress and furnishing, architecture, music and dancing, though still greater than in civilized countries, are becoming less marked. Foreign cloth was at first used in local idioms—Lozi women are distinguished by their full bustled skirts made after the fashion of the nineties when Paris missionaries first reached their country—but similar African fashions now spread over wide areas, and European dress is commonly worn. New styles of basket work are borrowed from neighbouring tribes—in 1936 Nyakyusa women were just learning to weave sleeping mats in what they called the Swahili pattern, quite different from their traditional style —and houses and furnishing of European design are appearing everywhere. In Broken Hill the less sophisticated dance traditional dances, each tribe its own, the Ila even bringing skins to stage their famous lion dance; but houseboys and clerks, irrespective of tribe, dance foxtrots and tangos in the cast-off clothes of their employers. All the towns have African dance clubs where foreign dances alone are performed.

Techniques are growing in elaboration and are being applied to more durable materials, while the accumulated technical skill of Europe is being increasingly mastered by Africans. The highly skilled are specialists.

Knowledge in the old societies was parochial and unspecialized. There was no writing, and though old men could recite genealogies of chiefs, and epics of victory or migration, they were ignorant of the everyday doings of their ancestors more than two generations back. Now the accumulated knowledge of a world society is spreading in

Central Africa. Schools organized by missions and Government are scattered throughout the three Territories. In Nyasaland nearly 50 % of the African children attend schools of some sort, in Northern Rhodesia about 36 %, in Tanganyika 18 %. But the percentage in schools of a reasonable degree of efficiency is considerably less—about 15 % in Nyasaland, 12 % in Northern Rhodesia, and 2·5 % in Tanganyika.[1] Nevertheless, the range of knowledge has

---

[1] These figures were arrived at as follows:

Children in School (Africans only)

Nyasaland (Report of Education Department, 1939—no detailed statistics given in 1940 and 1941 *Reports):*

In Government and aided schools	61,207
In unaided schools	145,244
Population	1,673,000
Percentage of population scholars	12·3 %
Percentage of population in aided schools	3·6 %

Northern Rhodesia (Native Education, Annual Report, 1939):

In Government and aided schools	42,674
In unaided schools	81,710
Population	1,366,425
Percentage of population scholars	9 %
Percentage in Government and aided schools	3·1 %

The Director of Education reports in 1942 that the enrolment has risen by approximately 100 % in Government and aided schools since 1939.

Tanganyika Territory (Report of the Education Department, 1937—no detailed statistics given in 1939 *Report):*

In Government and aided schools	31,150
In unaided schools	'Over 190,000 claimed'
Population	5,022,640
Percentage of population scholars	4·4 %
Percentage in Government and aided schools	0·62 %

Taking children of school age as 25 % of the population, the proportion of children in schools of any sort in Central Africa is then 26 %, in Government or aided schools 7 %.

The unaided schools are evangelistic centres maintained by Christian missions. According to the 1937 *Report of the Tanganyika Education Department,* 'It is not unfair to say that these institutions are for the most part housed in rude shacks, staffed by semi-literates, devoid of equipment, and lacking in competent supervision.'

extended enormously, both historically and geographically, and it is increasingly specialized.

It is obvious that the learning of common languages and the merging of dialects is correlated with the increase in trade and travel, but how far local styles can survive, and whether school education for Africans is necessitated by the new economic and political organization, are questions still hotly debated. Again the detailed connections between the different changes must be sought.

(iv) *Religious Changes*

In the primitive societies the gods were the ancestors or other spirits, whose influence was limited in range. Everyone practised magic and feared witchcraft, but the power of these was likewise limited. An enemy in a distant chiefdom was, to the Nyakyusa, for instance, beyond the range of supernatural vengeance, unless he were a relative. So too moral obligations normally extended only to neighbours, kinsmen, and fellow-subjects. Different families worshipped different ancestors, but there was a high degree of religious homogeneity in each society. Everyone acknowledged the power of the ancestors, of witches and of magic; eccentrics were not tolerated.

Now universal religions are spreading. The Europeans found Islam already established on the coast and along the main slave routes, but it is only since their coming that it has spread widely in the interior. In the last Nyasaland Census, 8 % of the population is returned as Mohammedan, and the percentage is probably much higher in Tanganyika,[1] but in Northern Rhodesia there are very few

---

[1] J. Richter, *Tanganyika and Its Future* (1934), gives 40% Mohammedan, but the accuracy of this is doubtful since he gives as his authority the 'Official census...in 1929', but according to the Government Printer, no census was taken in 1928 or 1929. There are no figures on religion in the most recent Tanganyika Native Census (1931).

Mohammedans. Christian missionaries have been active since the end of last century, and a substantial proportion of Africans now profess Christianity—over 10% in Northern Rhodesia,[1] 11% in Nyasaland as a whole,[2] but as much as 45% in one district, Ngonde.[3] Of the Nyakyusa in Tanganyika 15% were church members or adherents in 1939.[4] These converts are conscious of being members of world organizations. They contrast the range of their obligations with those of pagans, laying special emphasis on hospitality to strangers. Belief in ancestors and local spirits, in magic and in witchcraft, though still very vital, is observably declining, more and more diseases being ascribed to natural causes. There is considerable religious diversity. The degree in which people hold to the old religion varies, and of those who embrace new faiths not only do some acknowledge Jesus, and others Mohammed, but the Christians are divided into innumerable sects. Between pagan and non-pagan, Mohammedan and Christian, Catholic and Protestant, there is a measure of tolerance.

Again we look for connections between these and other changes. How far, we ask, does the economic change necessitate religious change? Is the diversity of belief a temporary phenomenon, or is it connected with the new economic and political organization? Many Europeans

[1] E. W. Smith, *The Way of the White Fields in Rhodesia* (1938), gives a total of 141,615 Christians. This figure includes communicants and catechumens of European-controlled churches, but not members of independent African churches.

[2] *Nyasaland Protectorate, Census Report*, 1931.

[3] Figures collected from the missionary in charge of the local mission, and from leaders of the independent African churches.

[4] J. Richter, *op. cit.*, gives a total of 307,017 'Baptised Christians' in Tanganyika (6% of the total population) in one table—his figures are not consistent. This excludes catechumens of whom complete figures are not given, and members of independent African churches. The figures on the Nyakyusa were collected from the supervisors of the various missions and independent African churches. Most Africans who profess Christianity are attached to some church.

express surprise at the tenacity of belief in magic and witchcraft; we seek the relation between this type of belief and the form of the society.

(c) SOCIAL ELEMENTS

Our second group of problems arises directly from the first. We ask ourselves whether the foregoing chronicle is, or is not, in principle complete. If it is, then understanding will come in the search for necessary connections between the facts already described; if it is not, then none of these facts can be fully understood, each being partly determined by unknown conditions.

To answer this question we must first know what are the elements of social relations—their universal constituents at all times and everywhere. The labours of economists have taught us to see economics as one such element, and have defined it for us with considerable precision; but there is neither precision in the definition of the other social elements, nor even agreement on their number and their names.

Only a precise definition of the social elements, moreover, and of their systematic interconnections, enables us to see clearly the necessary connections between our facts. The connection between the particular economy and the particular morality of modern Central Africa, for instance, points us back to some universal connection between economics and morality as such. Unless we see the universal connection clearly, the particular connection remains obscure.

In defining the social elements, we, being students of Central Africa, are bound to consider the widely differing facts of primitive and of modern civilized life. This leads us to hope that our definitions may be found applicable also to the intermediate facts of past civilizations. If they are not so applicable, then, of course, they fall to the ground.

(d) OPPOSITION AND MALADJUSTMENT

The society of Central Africa is marked by opposition and maladjustment. We seek the cause of this. Some suggest that uncontrollable opposition and maladjustment is normal in society;[1] others that it is necessarily involved in the change from primitive to civilized. Can it, we ask, be avoided, and if so how? An indication of the conditions that give rise to it is provided by the fact that it is not equally evident in all parts of Central Africa: it is far more evident in the industrial towns of Northern Rhodesia, for instance, than among the rural Nyakyusa.

There is a complex opposition usually called 'the race problem' which sets the subject African and the dominant European against one another, poises the small Indian group uneasily between them, and, within the European group itself, sets negrophil against negrophobe. Twice in five years Africans have rioted on the Northern Rhodesian copperbelt and been fired on by the military. Such influence as the Africans exert on Government policy conflicts with that exerted by the majority of the European immigrants, though European missionaries sometimes take the African side.

There is conflict between African and European industrial workers over the admission of the Africans to skilled jobs, and between African workers and European employers over wages. Both these conflicts were factors of the 1940 copperbelt riot, which was preceded by an African

[1] Cf. E. H. Carr, *The Twenty Years Crisis*; R. Niebuhr, *Moral Man and Immoral Society*.

strike. There is competition between European and African farmers for land and for markets. There is competition between European and African men for African women. There is a conflict, general in the urban areas of Northern Rhodesia, between the municipal and Government authorities on the one hand, and the Africans on the other, over the brewing of native beer. The authorities make it illegal either to brew or drink beer privately; they provide instead municipal beer-halls where it can be bought and drunk under supervision. The Africans, though they use the beer-halls, disapprove of the law, almost to a man, and brew beer freely. There is conflict between the Government and Africans over witchcraft. The Government makes it illegal for one man to accuse another of bewitching him, unless he can prove that there has been some open threat to do so. The Africans, most of whom still believe in the power of witchcraft, continue to accuse, and even to take action against one another, under the protecting silence of their own authorities.

Courtesy very markedly fails to govern the relations of the races in town, and less markedly in the country also. In Northern Rhodesia post offices and shops commonly provide separate entrances and a lower standard of courtesy for their African clients, who resent the differentiation, and sometimes push and clamour for attention. The increasing assumption by Africans of European dress and manners, though it symbolizes an increasing civilization, is accompanied by more rather than less discourtesy from many Europeans, who sense in it a bid for conventional equality.

To describe the character of this situation as a prevalent discourtesy is inadequate; it is rather an opposition of courtesies. Africans resent being passed over, but a shopman who should attend to an African in his turn when a European was waiting would be felt by the latter to have insulted him. To slight Africans is, in the European group, itself a convention, whose breach leads to embarrassment.

No small part of the race problem is an intellectual opposition which leads European and African to discuss the same things in contradictory terms. A discussion between members of the two groups about witchcraft, for instance, is usually a hopeless confusion: the one is discussing an unreality which people 'pretend' to detect and deal with, the other a terrible reality and the root of half his evils. Nor is it only the survival of primitive beliefs which makes for intellectual opposition; the everyday facts of the present situation are also differently conceived. To most Europeans an educated African is a savage, differing from his uneducated fellows only in that he is less picturesque, and less biddable; to himself the educated African is a civilized man. To some missionaries a pagan African is, in his family, a satanic influence; to the Christians of that family he is a respected relative. One of us discussed an African family in Broken Hill with a Catholic priest. The mother, a baptized Christian, had been married to a fellow Christian, who had deserted her after a few months. She then married a pagan who had now maintained her in comfort for sixteen years, and had children by her. By marrying him she became excommunicate. To the priest her present partner was still 'that pagan' who had seduced her from her Christian duty of remaining faithful to her first husband.

This opposition of the races is complicated by the fact that there is opposition within the European group itself over 'Native policy'; and within the African group between conservatives who would maintain traditional ways, and radicals who seek to approximate to Europeans in all things; between the young who buy fine clothes in town, and the old who go hungry in the country. Moreover,

Africans and Europeans are, for a second time, together involved in war against other Europeans and non-Europeans.

From many rural areas of Northern Rhodesia and Nyasaland, 30–50 % of the able-bodied men are always away at work[1], mostly in the industrial towns of Northern Rhodesia, in Southern Rhodesia, and the Union of South Africa. No proportionate number of the general population goes with them, and no proportionate flow of wealth comes back to balance their going. The majority of these so-called 'migrant labourers' now spend most of their working lives, and most of their wages, in town. In Broken Hill in 1940 it was found that 69·9 % of the total African labour force of 6,460 men had spent two-thirds of its time in town since first leaving the rural areas. It was also found that of the £67,830 annually received by them in

[1] In Northern Rhodesia, during 1940–1 the percentage of taxable males working outside their Province ranged between 3 and 50 %. In four out of seven Provinces it was over 30 %. The percentage of taxable males employed for wages, and therefore not free for agricultural and other duties at home, ranged from 33 to 62 % (*Northern Rhodesia, Labour Department, Annual Report*, 1941).

The Committee on Emigrant Labour in Nyasaland estimated that 120,000 men or 'more than a quarter of the adult male population' was absent from the Territory in 1935 (*Nyasaland Protectorate, Report on Emigrant Labour*, 1935, p. 15). In 1940 the number was estimated to be 101,800 (*Nyasaland Protectorate, Annual Report of the Labour Department*, 1940). The proportion working outside their home districts must be still higher. Dr Read found from 14 to 75 % (average 35 %) away in the villages she investigated in 1939 (Article on 'Migrant Labour in Africa' in *International Labour Review*, June 1942, pp. 617–19).

In Tanganyika the proportion of men away at work is known to be much smaller, though no figures are available. The number of men estimated to leave their *districts* (not Province) in search of work in 1940 was 0·65 % of the total population of these districts at the last Census (*Tanganyika Territory, Labour Department, Annual Report*, 1940—estimate for four out of eight Provinces only). In Nyasaland the number of men estimated to leave the *Protectorate* in 1940 was 2·4 % of the total population (*Nyasaland Protectorate, Annual Report of the Labour Department*, 1940). This suggests that the percentage of men absent from their districts in Tanganyika is less than a third of those absent from the Protectorate in Nyasaland.

cash wages,[1] only 17·7 % (£12,033) was returned in any form to their rural homes. Of this total, £4,880 was returned for their own use on visits home. Thus only 10·5 % (£7,153), i.e. about 22s. per man per year, was passed on to their rural dependents.

In Broken Hill there were 7,500 men, nearly all able-bodied. With the men were 3,500 women and 4,000 children. The men, that is, were half the urban population. Of a normal population able-bodied men are about a fifth. Thus for every dependent they had in town with them three were left in the country. Yet they and their few urban dependents consumed nine-tenths of their cash wages, as well as their quarters and rations. The 'equilibrium' postulated by economists does not exist in this situation; the country gives to the towns far more than it gets from them.

Most of the men in town are young. The average age of the men in Broken Hill was 24 years 7 months, and their average age on leaving the rural areas was just under 16 years. 41·2 % of them were not married. Nevertheless, they had dependents.[2] The young unmarried men are essential to the country economy (*vide infra*, pp. 142–3).

In many rural areas, denuded of able-bodied men, agriculture is declining and malnutrition increasing;[3] houses are not repaired and the villages have a desolate air.[4] No efforts of the remaining men, the women and the children can make up for the absence of the younger men, for there has not been an improvement in agricultural

[1] Cash wages are less than half the real wages which usually include quarters and some rations in kind.

[2] Godfrey Wilson, *The Economics of Detribalization in Northern Rhodesia*, part I, Rhodes-Livingstone Papers No. 5, 1941, pp. 36–47.

[3] Cf. Margaret Read, 'Native standards of living and African culture change', Supplement to *Africa*, Vol. XI, No. 3, 1938, pp. 21, 36–45.

[4] Cf. A. I. Richards, *Land, Labour and Diet in Northern Rhodesia*, 1939, pp. 404–5.

technique such as to enable those who remain to increase their production. Indeed, there is evidence of an actual decline in agricultural skill in some areas.[1] Young Bemba are less skilled in choosing soils than their fathers: Africans as well as Europeans complain of the unskilfulness of modern village agriculture.[2]

The economic maladjustment is far less evident in Tanganyika. It is also less evident in some of the rural areas of Northern Rhodesia and Nyasaland than in others. In these areas the disproportion of the population is slight; many of the men stay at home growing food for the towns, or export crops, as well as food for themselves. In Tanganyika Africans produce for export, cotton, coffee, rice, hides, ghee, beeswax, copra, groundnuts and tobacco, besides supplying considerable quantities of food for the local market. This is a contrast to Nyasaland, from which the only African-grown products exported in appreciable quantities are cotton and tobacco; and to Northern Rhodesia, from which Africans export only beeswax, and in some seasons, maize.[3] In Northern Rhodesia, moreover, the local market for food is largely supplied by European farmers.

The increased production in Tanganyika is made possible by improvements in agricultural technique. The Nyakyusa supply not only labour to the adjacent Lupa goldfields, but also food; and they sell rice and coffee on the world market. A substantial proportion of their able-

[1] C. G. Trapnell and J. K. Clothier, 'Soils, Vegetations and Agricultural Systems of North Western Rhodesia'. *Report of the Ecological Survey*, Lusaka, 1937, p. 61.

[2] Richards, *op. cit.* pp. 286–7.

[3] Cf. Agricultural Reports for the three Territories. No complete figures on African production are available, for in the figures of exports European and African produce are not always distinguished, and of local trade there is often no record. Since the war Northern Rhodesia has developed a trade in baskets with the Union.

bodied men is always away; but the use of ploughs, and the combination of coffee with bananas, which gives a double crop with comparatively little extra labour, has made it possible for those who remain to increase their production sufficiently to provide food for everyone and a balance for export.

The transfer of wealth from town to country is also greater in some areas than in others. From Broken Hill a considerably greater proportion of wages was taken back to the nearer, than to the distant, rural areas;[1] and Nyakyusa prosperity partly depended on the fact that they lived near the Lupa goldfields, worked for short periods, and took most of their earnings home. Dr Read tells of the relative prosperity of a Nyasa village from which 75 % of the men were away, but to which they brought or sent back money regularly.[2]

Erosion is a major problem in Central Africa. Nyasaland is said to be incapable of supporting one-half of the population that it supported a hundred years ago,[3] owing to deforestation and erosion; and in some parts of Tanganyika, and Northern Rhodesia also, erosion is serious.[4] Not only has competition between European and African for land reduced the areas available for African cultivation, but the demand for export crops and the introduction of the plough, has increased the areas cultivated, and reduced the period allowed for recovery.[5] Thus export crops, while temporarily relieving the poverty of the country, may, if not carefully controlled, eventually increase it. It is, how-

[1] Godfrey Wilson, *op. cit.* part i, p. 66.

[2] Margaret Read, *International Labour Review,* June 1942, pp. 619, 622.

[3] ♪ J. W. Hornby, 'Denudation and Soil Erosion in Nyasaland'. *Nyasaland Department of Agriculture,* Bulletin No. 11, 1934.

[4] Lord Hailey, *An African Survey,* pp. 1087–93.

[5] It is not known whether or not there has been an increase in the African population of Central Africa during the last hundred years (Hailey, *op. cit.* pp. 112–25). It is thought that it is declining in Northern Rhodesia.

ever, noticeable that Nyasaland, where erosion is most acute, exports little African-grown produce, nor has it exported much in the past; and some exporting districts, such as BuNyakyusa, are not eroded at all.

Preventable ill-health is known to be widespread—over 90 % of the population has been found to be infected with one or more kinds of worms in some areas—but there is no exact knowledge of the extent of disease. It is, however, generally agreed that malnutrition is the main factor in causing ill-health.[1]

The learning of one another's languages and the growth of *linguae francae* has not kept pace with the need. Africans speaking many different languages are thrown into relations with one another, and with Indians and Europeans, and are often only superficially acquainted with any common medium. The constant friction between European mistresses and African domestic servants is often due to misunderstanding. In the courts, too, linguistic difficulties are serious.

To the European the African is not only unskilful, he is also ignorant. That Africans themselves find their knowledge inadequate for their needs is proved by their eagerness for schooling. Many an adult painfully learns the alphabet from a literate friend, after the day's work is over.

There is a profound religious maladjustment in that incompatible values are pursued, and incompatible dogmas maintained, by people in close relations with one another. Many of the Europeans pursue the exclusive values of race, and believe that those who are not racially exclusive are doing evil. To them the hand-shaking missionary is a traitor, who undermines the prestige of the white race. On the other hand, many Africans have accepted Christianity, and interpret it as being all-inclusive. To them the doctrine

[1] Hailey, *op. cit.* pp. 1115–52.

of brotherly love and the colour bar appear contradictory. 'He was a really good man', two Africans said wonderingly to us in Broken Hill, 'he preached a splendid sermon on brotherly love; you could see in his face as he spoke that he was a good man. Yet when we went to see him he kept us waiting and then came out of the house to us: he would not ask us in.' Many European Christians reconcile the doctrines of race and of Christianity[1] without apparent difficulty, worshipping in churches from which fellow-Christians are excluded on the ground of colour. Others, finding the values incompatible, are forced into an uneasy compromise. Humanists are involved in similar contradictions.

Among the Africans themselves, the most obvious instance of religious maladjustment is the combined pursuit of sexual satisfaction and of stability and fidelity in marriage, under conditions that largely exclude their combined realization. The great predominance of men in the towns, and of women in many of the country districts, makes it impossible for a very large number of people to obtain sexual satisfaction save by extra-marital adventures. Sexual satisfaction, none the less, continues to be pursued. Unsatisfied bachelors and grass widowers in town press adulterous attentions on the married women, and open to those willing to adopt it a profitable career as prostitutes. Deserted wives and unpledged girls in the country often find the prospect of a transient liaison overwhelmingly alluring.

Yet very few Africans judge the adultery, the frequent divorce, the prostitution, and concubinage that results, to be anything but evil. They deplore it as do the Europeans. Sexual satisfaction is held good: the steps by which alone it can often be attained are held evil.

---

[1] 94% of the Europeans resident in Northern Rhodesia professed themselves Christian in the Census of 1931. A much smaller proportion is attached to any church.

Such is the maladjustment that the very efforts of men and women to maintain the chastity which they continue to value often have an effect just the opposite of that intended. Sexual immorality is most pronounced in towns. In the country the surplus women usually live under the eyes of older relatives, whose influence continually presses on them the obligations either of a traditional, or of a new Christian, morality. Parents, elders and chiefs therefore—the moral leaders of the countryside—often restrain women from going to town lest they be corrupted.[1] But the main cause of the immorality is the disproportion of the sexes in town and country. Every woman who is restrained from going to town makes sexual immorality, both in town and country, so much the more inevitable.

(c) The Paradox of Incoherence

These oppositions and maladjustments face us with a paradox. All objective analysis of social relations rests on the assumption that they form coherent systems, that within any one field they support and determine one another inexorably. The oppositions and maladjustments we have just catalogued, however, show us a field in which social relations are largely incoherent, pulling against and contradicting one another.

The general problem then is to resolve this paradox, for we cannot deny either of its terms. To deny the assumption of social coherence would be to abandon all hope of analysis in history, and to fall back on mere chronicle of seemingly accidental and so incomprehensible events. To ignore the observable incoherencies would be to abandon that fidelity to facts from which alone historical analysis can begin.

[1] Cf. *Nyasaland Protectorate, Report on Emigrant Labour*, 1935, p. 27. Native opinion is against wives going to town 'because, the location and mine compounds are generally bad places for women'.

CHAPTER II

SCALE

THE difference between the traditional societies of Central Africa and modern Central African society is, in one respect, a difference of size. Comparatively few people were in close relations in the old societies, and their characteristics were correlates of their smallness of scale; many people are in close relations in the modern society, and its characteristics are correlates of its largeness of scale. That difference of scale is a fundamental difference between primitive and civilized society has long been recognized, but the concept has lacked precision. We seek to refine it.

(a) THE BOUNDARIES OF SOCIETY

Society is always universal in the sense that living people everywhere are always involved, however indirectly, with all other living people and with all past generations since the emergence of man. Until recently, however, it has never been universal in the sense that all these relations have been in any degree directly realized, that is, have been sufficiently intense for men to be aware of their positive content (*vide infra*, pp. 45–8). The extent of conscious relations, contemporary and historical, is the extent of a particular society. Only quite recently has any particular society approached universality. We to-day are conscious of relations between past groups of which they themselves knew nothing.

Societies overlap and shade into one another. The men of primitive Ngonde had direct contacts with the Bemba,

but not with the more distant Lala; the Bemba had direct
contacts both with Ngonde and with the Lala. Thus
Bemba society included both the Lala and Ngonde, while
Ngonde society included the Bemba only. Every society
must be given a point of reference before it can be defined.
When we speak of 'Nyakyusa society' or 'Central African
society' we include all the relations directly realized by the
Nyakyusa, and by the inhabitants of Central Africa,
respectively.

(b) CRITERIA OF SCALE

By the scale of a society we mean the number of people
in relation and the intensity of those relations. Modern
Central African society is larger in scale than those which
preceded it, not only because more people are in conscious
relations with one another, but also because the relations
between Africa and the outside world, and between contemporary Africans and long past generations, are more
intense than they were. In comparing the scale of societies
therefore, we compare the relative size of groups with
relations of similar intensity.

The members of all societies are equally dependent upon
one another, but the range of their interdependence varies
geographically and historically. A Bushman, we maintain,
is as dependent upon his fellows as an Englishman, but the
Englishman depends upon many more people than does
the Bushman. The Englishman gets his food from the four
quarters of the globe, and is directly affected by the ideas
of twenty-five centuries. The Bushman depends for food
only upon his immediate neighbours, and is affected by
the ideas of past generations only in so far as they are
communicated to him by those elders whose life overlaps
with his. The total degree of interdependence, or intensity
of relations, is the same, but in the case of the Englishman

it is more spread out. The intensity of particular relations varies in different societies, but the total intensity of all the relations of society does not. It follows, therefore, that as the range of relations increases, the degree of dependence upon neighbours and contemporaries diminishes.[1]

The intensity of relations in a given group is to be measured by the intensity of co-operation,[2] and of intellectual and emotional communication, both contemporary and historical. That is:

(i) By the proportion of economic co-operation within that group to the total economic co-operation of the society, whether that co-operation is with contemporaries in the form of joint production, or exchange through trade and reciprocal gifts; or with past generations through the use of capital inherited from them. The area of close economic co-operation in primitive societies is much smaller than in civilized society, and the capital inherited from past generations is also smaller.

(ii) By the proportion of communication of fact in speech and writing, within that group, to the total intellectual communication of the society. The area of communication is necessarily smaller in an illiterate society than in a literate one. Primitives often have little knowledge of what is going on a hundred miles away, and oral traditions beyond the memory of the oldest inhabitants are meagre.

(iii) By the proportion of emotional expression communicated within that group to the total expression of the society. In primitive societies communication of feeling barely extends beyond personal contacts, for there is no

---

[1] Here we part company with Durkheim. He postulates an increase in 'density' (i.e. in intensity of relations) with increase in scale. He overlooked the fact that as density increases between the previously separate 'segments' it decreases within them. Cf. E. Durkheim, *De la Division du Travail Social.*

[2] War is included in co-operation.

literary art, and each small group being largely self-sufficient, the manufactured articles which circulate are few. Historically, it is also limited by the absence of written records and of lasting mediums. In civilized society, on the other hand, books and musical scores, tools, utensils and pictures travel far and wide, and are inherited from generations long past.

(iv) By the relative value set on contemporary co-operation and continuity within and without the group. In primitive societies co-operation within small local groups was valued; co-operation with distant groups was not. In civilized society, on the other hand, loyalty to large political groups is a value constantly pursued. Religious inclusiveness is limited by race, nation and class, but a universal society is valued by some. Christians praise neighbourly behaviour even between Jews and Samaritans; Communists appeal for the unity of the workers of the world.

All societies value continuity, but the period over which it is valued varies. In primitive society the period is limited by the absence of traditions going back more than ten or twelve generations.[1] Civilized societies, on the other hand, boast of the continuity between their institutions, topics of discussion and modes of expression and those of the ancient world. By *continuity* we mean both the volume of material co-operation and communication with the past, and the non-material unity that exists when people act, speak and feel as if it were a reality. This non-material continuity is differently defined in different societies. Primitives tend to define it as cultural similarity, and stress observance of the *same* customs as were practised by their fathers. In modern society it is development which is stressed—there is held to be a certain continuity between feudalism and modern

[1] E. E. Evans-Pritchard, *The Nuer*, p. 108. Cf. Nyakyusa evidence, p. 32.

constitutional government, not because both are alike, but because one grew out of the other[1] (*vide infra*, pp. 101–8).

(v) By the relative degree of unity and continuity dogmatically asserted within and without the group. Small groups often emphasize their common descent, larger groups their common race, others their common humanity, thus expressing both present unity and continuity with the past. Or the common bond emphasized may be cultural homogeneity. Literate groups, having greater historical knowledge, trace their common descent or common culture through more generations than illiterate groups.

(vi) By the degree in which a sense of unity and continuity is expressed within the group, compared to that expressed with outsiders. Unity and continuity are expressed in a common name, a common style of dress, a common flag, or, as Professor Radcliffe-Brown has shown in his classical exposition,[2] through common myths and ceremonies. The way in which the area of application of a common symbol increases as intensity of relations increases is illustrated by the traditional and modern use of the name *Nyakyusa*. Traditionally it applied to a few chiefdoms on the north shore of Lake Nyasa. Neighbouring groups of similar culture, with whom relations were tenuous, called themselves the people of Selya, of Kukwe, and of Mwamba. Now all three groups are in close relations and commonly refer to themselves as Nyakyusa.[3] In civilized society the group using a common symbol, such as a name, extends much further historically, as well as geographically, than in primitive society.

(vii) By the degree of social pressure exerted within the

---

[1] Cf. G. M. Trevelyan, *History of England*, p. 167.

[2] A. R. Radcliffe-Brown, *The Andaman Islanders*, Chaps. v and vi.

[3] We use 'Nyakyusa' in its modern sense, and 'Nyakyusa proper' for the smaller group.

group compared with that exerted on and by outsiders. The more intense the relations between individuals or groups the greater the mutual pressure they exert on each other. In primitive societies power is exercised only within a comparatively small group. The area in which any ruler can exert pressure by force of arms, and in which law is effective, is limited. The range of power in time is as limited as it is in space. Legal decisions are made in accordance with precedents, but since there are no written records the cases cited are necessarily comparatively recent. Ancestors are believed to have power over men, but it is the immediate ancestors who are feared. Similarly, logical and conventional pressure are exerted only within a small group. A man is not influenced by the arguments of those living at a distance or those long dead. He fears the scorn and enjoys the admiration only of neighbours and contemporaries.

In civilized societies the range of social pressure is much greater. The military power of large groups extends over the world, and law is effective over wide areas. Through written codes and records of case law, generations long dead directly affect contemporary law. The values of Christ, of Buddha and of Mohammed directly affect behaviour to-day—it is not only his immediate predecessors who have moral power over a civilized man. Similarly, his thoughts and feelings are shaped by those far from him in space and time.

We measure the intensity of relations within a group, then, by observing the proportion of economic co-operation, of communication of ideas and of feelings within and without the group; together with the relative inclusiveness of value, of dogma and of symbolism within and without the group, and the degree of social pressure exerted within and without the group.

Groups and individuals within the same society differ in the range and intensity of their relations. In Central Africa, for example, the Europeans are in more intense relations with the outside world than the Africans, and an educated Swahili is similarly wider in scale in his relations than a conservative Nyakyusa. The proportion of the population that is wide scale in their relations is another measure of intensity in the wider relations. It *is* the relative intensity of the wider relations compared with the narrower.

These criteria of intensity cannot of course be measured with mathematical precision: we seek only a means of comparing relative intensity. The reasons for our choice of these criteria are explained in the next chapter.

The intensity of relations, be it noted, is distinguished from cultural similarity; for there may, at any moment, be considerable cultural similarity due to close co-operation and communication with a common parent society, but little present co-operation and communication, as when sections of tribes (such as the Makololo and Ngoni) left their traditional homes and settled at a far distance from their relatives, but retained much of their traditional culture.

(c) The Boundaries of Community

Within society are *communities*, which, like society, we define historically as well as geographically.[1] Communities are areas and periods of common life of more or less intensity. To facilitate the comparison of scale we distinguish between the largest community and extra-communal relations. The boundaries of community are the boundaries of many-sided relationship; extra-communal relations are one-sided and

[1] Cf. Evans-Pritchard's brilliant analysis of the correlation between contemporary and historical scale, *op. cit.* pp. 106–7.

tenuous. The boundaries of community, like those of society, vary with the point of reference, and the exact line of demarcation is not always clear, but in cases in which the relevant facts are known it can be defined as falling within certain narrow limits.

Historically, circles of community are always interlocking; geographically they may be interlocking or discrete. That is to say, if we take a point of reference *A*, and *B* is a point on the boundary of community *A*, the boundaries of community *B* may or may not coincide with those of community *A*. Community *B* may include only part of the area of community *A*, and also part of a third area, community *C*.

Among the Nyakyusa, for example, community did not extend from any particular point of reference beyond the neighbouring chiefdoms and the lifetime of the oldest inhabitants. Historically, these circles were interlocking; geographically, they were at least partially discrete. At some points communities were separated by physical barriers, such as the wall of the Livingstone Mountains between the Nyakyusa and Kinga, and the uninhabited forest belt between Selya and the Nyakyusa proper, and therefore did not interlock; but we do not think that all the boundaries of groups of neighbouring chiefdoms were as difficult to cross as these. On this point we lack evidence.

The main productive unit of the Nyakyusa[1] was the individual family. Circulation of wealth was chiefly in the form of marriage gifts; and marriage, though most frequent within the chiefdom, occurred fairly often between neighbouring chiefdoms, but not between distant ones. Beyond the neighbouring chiefdoms there was trade in iron, salt, a red dye, and cloth, which were exchanged for cattle,

[1] For a short account of the Nyakyusa see Godfrey Wilson, 'An introduction to Nyakyusa Society', *Bantu Studies*, Sept. 1936.

food and ivory; but the volume of this trade was very small indeed, and it was usually mediated by neighbours. Only the people of chiefdoms next to the Kinga, the producers of the red dye, bought straight from them, and they in turn sold it only to neighbouring chiefdoms. There was no coming and going of traders between distant chiefdoms. Cattle raids also were made only against neighbouring chiefdoms.

Capital was inherited in the form of cattle, seed, a few tools, certain knowledge and skills, and rights over land. This involved a degree of co-operation with distant ancestors—the domesticators of cattle, the first agriculturalists and inventors, the original occupants of the land—but relations with these creators of their cultural heritage were not directly realized. Such legends as there are of the beginnings of Nyakyusa culture are put but ten generations back. Fire, for example, is said to have been brought by the chiefs who, ten generations ago, descended from the Livingstone Mountains and conquered the previous inhabitants of the Nyakyusa valley. Until then the men of the valley had eaten their food raw.

Not only were the Nyakyusa unaware of relations extending more than ten generations back, but the volume of capital inherited was small compared with that in a civilized society, and men were wholly dependent for it on the immediately preceding generation. They did not inherit buildings and roads and irrigation schemes, made by distant ancestors about whom they knew, as do civilized men.

There was no writing, and so intellectual communication was largely confined to personal contacts which rarely extended beyond the neighbouring chiefdoms. As we have seen traditions going back ten generations existed—old men recited genealogies and told of battles lost and won—but the facts known about generations beyond living memory were few. For example, of the numbers and culture of the conquerors who came down from the Livingstones ten generations ago, and of the previous occupants of the valley, the Nyakyusa know nothing. It is difficult even to discover details of everyday life before the coming of the Europeans in 1891.

Communication of feeling was also mainly through personal contacts and confined to neighbouring chiefdoms and overlapping generations. Dancing was among the chief mediums of expression and people did not attend dances beyond the circle within which they married. Each tiny group was, as we have seen, largely self-sufficient; the only manufactured goods traded beyond neighbouring chiefdoms were iron tools and weapons and cloth, and the quantity of these was very small. Elton (the first European to travel through the country) speaks of rarely seeing cloth in 1877,[1] and even in 1936 in remote districts the use of iron hoes was still confined to men, women using digging sticks, though near the Government station women too used iron hoes.

There were no lasting mediums except iron, baked clay, and hard wood; and since iron was scarce, clay pots shattered, and hard wood was little used, the works of art passing down the generations were as few as those circulated beyond neighbouring chiefdoms. Where the circles of community interlocked geographically, tales and dances and songs may have travelled far in space as they did in time—the great similarity of folk tales over Bantu Africa proves that they travelled at least one way—but without writing and choreography and musical scores the volume of art thus circulated was necessarily limited. What was forgotten by one generation was lost for good.

[1] J. F. Elton, *Travels and Researches among the Lakes and Mountains of Eastern and Central Africa* (1879), pp. 316, 320, 322, 331.

The Nyakyusa valued co-operation within the group of neighbouring chiefdoms, but not beyond it. They held that it was best to marry within the chiefdom, allowable to marry in a neighbouring chiefdom, but not good to marry at a distance. So too it was continuity with the customs of their fathers, rather than with those of distant ancestors, that was insisted upon. Since tradition did not go back further than ten generations the range of continuity valued at all was short. Whether the heroes whose names and adventures are remembered actually lived only ten generations ago is here irrelevant; beyond that, continuity was neither conceived nor valued.

The unity of groups of neighbouring chiefdoms and their distinction from others, was further asserted in a dogma of common descent—the chiefs of Selya were closely related, as were those of the Kukwe, and of the Nyakyusa proper—and expressed in a common ritual, the chief of the senior line in each group sacrificing on its behalf. This dogmatic and ritual unity applied to the groups of neighbouring chiefdoms in Selya, among the Kukwe, and the Nyakyusa proper, respectively. Thus, in so far as Nyakyusa communities were discrete, the unity of each was expressed in dogma and ritual; in so far as they were geographically interlocking, the unity of border communities was not so expressed (*vide supra*, p. 31).

These same dogmas and rituals asserted and symbolized unity with near, rather than with more distant ancestors. One of us attended a ritual in Selya to which the junior chief of the group, who traditionally should have sent a cow to be killed by the senior, refused to do so, on the ground that 'the relationship was now distant'.

Relationship was also asserted beyond the boundaries of community. Between the chiefs of Selya and the Nyakyusa proper it was actually traced, but it was much more distant than within each group. Between the chiefs of the Kukwe and other Nyakyusa, and between the Nyakyusa, the people of Ngonde, the Ndali, the Kinga, the Bena and the Hehe, it was believed to exist, but no one could trace it. The people of Selya, the Nyakyusa proper, and the Kinga were further linked by a common ritual sacrificing to a reputed common ancestor, Lwembe, but these bonds were not in themselves sufficient to create community between groups who scarcely traded or intermarried, and who knew little about one another.

The range of social pressure was likewise limited. Law was effective within each tiny chiefdom of 100 to 3,000 men, and was sometimes applied to cases between members of neighbouring chiefdoms. It did not apply to strangers from a distance unless they were under the special protection of the chief, or of a member of the chiefdom. Men of Selya feared to travel even to Tukuyu twenty-five miles away, for strangers were liable to be assaulted and robbed, and had no redress.

It was only within and between neighbouring chiefdoms, also, that there was war. Funeral dances were a common occasion of dispute. When a man went to the funeral of his kinsmen in a neighbouring chiefdom, the young men of his own chiefdom often accompanied him armed, and joined in the dancing. They danced as a group showing off before the girls of the other chiefdom, and doing everything they could to appear fiercer and braver than their rivals. In this electric situation, charged with the memory of past fights and rivalries, insults were often hurled, and then another fight would occur.[1] Attendance at funerals, however, did not extend beyond the circle within which men married, and therefore this occasion for war only occurred

---

[1] Godfrey Wilson, 'Nyakyusa conventions of burial', p. 14, *Bantu Studies*, March 1939.

between members of neighbouring chiefdoms. One or two Ngoni and Sango raids are remembered, but neither Ngoni nor Sango entered Nyakyusa country in force, and their raids were few.

Supernatural sanctions were believed to be effective only against kinsmen, neighbours, and those with whom a man was in personal contact. No one feared witchcraft from outside the chiefdom.[1] Historically, also, it was those who were near who were feared. A commoner only made offerings to immediately past generations; and even chiefs, whose genealogies were better remembered, and who sacrificed to more remote ancestors, sacrificed more frequently to their fathers and grandfathers. In the prayers of chiefs and commoners alike the names of the ancestors were invoked in ascending order.

With relations so tenuous, neither the arguments of those beyond neighbouring chiefdoms, nor their conventions, could influence men, any more than could their laws.

There was then considerable intensity of relations within the area of neighbouring Nyakyusa chiefdoms, and between overlapping generations, but beyond this relations were tenuous and one-sided. With some distant chiefdoms there was a tradition of common descent, and occasionally a common ritual; with others there was a small volume of trade; with the Ngoni and Sango there was occasional war; but with no distant group was there many-sided relationship. With generations beyond living memory there was a degree of religious unity appearing in morality, dogma and ritual, but little economic co-operation with them, and little knowledge of them. But few works of art were inherited from them. Nyakyusa community, therefore, did not extend beyond living memory and neighbouring chiefdoms, though Nyakyusa society went back ten

[1] Godfrey Wilson, 'An African morality', *Africa*, Jan. 1936, p. 91.

generations and included the people[1] within an area of perhaps 5,000 square miles, Ngoni raiders, and Arab traders.

The boundaries of community were somewhat wider geographically in Ngonde than among the Nyakyusa: not only was the circle of extra-communal relations wider, but relations with the Arabs, though still one-sided, were much more intense than they were between Nyakyusa and Arab. Ngonde trade in ivory was considerable. In the historical moment also the scale was correspondingly greater.[2] Bemba society was likewise larger in scale than Nyakyusa society.[3]

Although the traditional societies of Central Africa differed thus in scale, the differences between them were, however, slight compared with the difference between the largest of them and modern Central African society. Taking England as the point of reference, community now extends geographically over practically the whole world— only a few remote tribes, such as those in Central New Guinea and on the Amazon, are excluded from it—and historically for well over 2,000 years. Central Africa, though not yet in as close relations with the outside world or with past generations as is England, is already within the circle of universal community.

As we have seen, Central Africa trades with the world and is seriously affected by fluctuations in the world market; capital accumulated by past generations, including the vast body of knowledge and skill handed down through

[1] Taking Selya as the point of reference these were: the Kinga, the Kesi, the Bena, the Hehe, the Safwa, the Poroto, the Nyika, the Penja, the Lambia, the Ndali, the Sango, and the men of Ngonde; as well as the Kukwe, the Mwamba and the Nyakyusa proper.

[2] Godfrey Wilson, *The Constitution of Ngonde*.

[3] Audrey Richards, *op. cit.* and essay on 'The political system of the Bemba tribe' in *African Political Systems* (edited Fortes and Evans-Pritchard), 1940.

many literate generations, is invested there. It is in communication with the world, and, through its literate inhabitants who read the Bible and the Koran and who are beginning to study history, with distant generations. Manufactured goods and works of art from the five continents circulate—cloth from Japan, books from Europe, films from America, tennis racquets from Australia—and so do the music and books and pictures of long past generations. It is common to hear the psalms of David, or a Bach choral, or to see a copy of a Renaissance Madonna in a remote African church.

With the spread of universal religions the range of morality has extended. Christians praise co-operation with all men, Mohammedans with their fellow-believers, and both seek inspiration from prophets and saints long dead. Communists, too, value co-operation on a universal scale, and though their great prophets are within living memory yet they value the continuity between their struggles and those of revolutionaries throughout the ages. So, too, in dogma and symbol the unity of universal groups are expressed. The Christian celebrates All Saints' Day, the Mohammedan the fast of Ramadan, the Communist his May Day, all remembering both the living and the dead of their faith.

Nevertheless, religious inclusiveness is still limited by nationality, race and class. Interracial marriage, for example, is as much discouraged in Central Africa to-day as was marriage with distant chiefdoms by the Nyakyusa.

Law is effective, during peace time, over most of the world. Were it not that the person and property of foreigners were protected there could be no international trade and travel, 'Violations of . . . (international) law are extremely rare. . . . The common impression to the contrary arises from the unfortunate concentration of popular interest on the laws of war, and a consequent failure to observe that the less sensational but far more important part of the system, the laws of peace, is constantly and unobtrusively observed in the daily intercourse of states.'[1] War, like law, is on a world scale, and thought and feeling are shaped by those distant in space and time.

(d) COMPARABLE GROUPS

We have argued that in comparing the scale of societies it is necessary to compare the range of groups with relations of similar intensity, and to facilitate comparison we have distinguished communities, groups with more intense relations, from extra-communal relations, the less intense relations of society. The relative scale of a society from any given point of reference may then be judged by (a) the relative number of people living and dead in conscious relation, and (b) the relative number of people living and dead in community. Modern Central African society includes the population of the world and all the past generations of which we are aware. Nyakyusa society included perhaps 250,000 souls and ten past generations. The modern Central African community includes very nearly the whole population of the world and perhaps 7,000 generations; a Nyakyusa community included perhaps 30,000 of the living and those who had died within their memory.

This is, of course, only a very rough measure of relative scale, for the degree of community between distant groups may be greater or less, and the degree of intensity of extra-communal relations greater or less. Of two societies with equal numbers in conscious relation and in community,

[1] J. L. Brierly, *The Law of Nations*, p. 51.

that in which the wider relations are more intense is larger in scale.

(e) INCREASE IN SCALE

Increase in the scale of a society may be by an increase in the numbers in relation through increase in population, exploration, or historical and archaeological discovery; or by an increase in the intensity of the more tenuous relations. In the modern world geographical expansion has practically reached its limit, but there may be an increase in scale not only through increase in population and the discovery by archaeologists of previously unknown societies, but also through an increase in the intensity of the relations between races and classes, and between the present and the past. It is also possible that, if wars continue, the scale of modern society may diminish (*vide infra*, p. 173).

Our hypothesis is that the total degree of dependence upon others, i.e. the intensity of relations, is the same in all societies, but that it may be more or less spread out. Intensity in the narrower circles of relation necessarily diminishes as intensity in the wider circles increases.

Our examples so far have been framed to show increasing intensity in the wider relations, but the same facts may illustrate decreasing intensity in the narrower relations. In a small-scale society a man is wholly dependent upon his immediate circle of contemporaries for food; there may be plenty in one district and famine across the mountains; plenty in one season and famine in the next. In a civilized society men are not so dependent upon neighbours, for food comes from the ends of the earth, and in times of famine they may draw upon capital accumulated by their ancestors to buy from a distance.

Similarly, a civilized man is less dependent upon his neighbours and contemporaries intellectually and emotionally than a primitive. He reads books written by those living at a distance and those long dead; he enjoys the music of Bach or Beethoven on wireless and gramophone, and the films of America and Europe; while the primitive has no choice but the conversation and songs of his fellow-villagers. In an illiterate society without lasting mediums men are wholly dependent upon overlapping generations for the knowledge and techniques they inherit. What is not passed on during the lifetime of the wise and skilled is lost, for there can be no rediscovery of ancient manuscripts and works of art.

The corollary of this is that local patriotism declines as wider loyalties develop, and emphasis on the worship of immediate ancestors diminishes with increase in historical range. The civic sense is not as strong in a modern borough as in a city state; nor is the unity of the kinship group as great in England as in a primitive society. A civilized man who put his town or his family before his state would be judged wrong by his fellows, though one who puts his state before some wider group is still usually judged to be right. A pagan Nyakyusa believes himself to be dependent upon his deceased father for health and fertility; he acts as if he were, and expresses his sense of dependence in rituals. A civilized man does not believe himself to be so dependent upon his immediate ancestors, but claims to follow the teaching of Christ or Confucius; Buddha, Mohammed or Marx. That Marx lived last century is from this point of view accidental—he may well be honoured many genera-tions hence. Greater autonomy in the narrower relations as well as greater subordination in the wider, is thus an aspect of the increase in scale.

(f) SCALE AND ENVIRONMENT

Certain environmental conditions tend towards largeness of scale, others towards smallness of scale. Where navigable water and healthy open country make transport easy, societies are likely to be larger in scale than where communications are physically difficult. In Africa physical conditions have tended towards isolation. The coastline is short and lacks good harbours; navigable rivers are few. Violent climatic differences also hindered travel. The Nyakyusa told us many tales of how, in the old days, men died of cold when they tried to cross the 8,000-foot range which blocks the Nyakyusa valley to the north. The difference between the hot steamy atmosphere of the valley, and the cold of the hills, was too great to be borne by unclothed and malaria-infected men. Nyakyusa still fear to visit the adjoining Kinga who live on top of the Livingstone Mountains on their eastern boundary, lest they die of cold, and of spirrulum tick fever, which is endemic among the Kinga but uncommon in the Nyakyusa valley. When we made the journey two Nyakyusa of our party did in fact suffer severely from tick fever. Environmental conditions explain why the Nyakyusa remained isolated and smaller scale than Ngonde or Bemba. Their valley was enclosed on three sides by high ranges, and on the fourth side by the stormy waters of Nyasa. The north tip of the lake, being in a funnel between high mountains, is liable to very severe squalls, which are feared even by steamers.

Similar barriers to communication existed elsewhere. Evans-Pritchard reports that the Galla and Amhara of the Ethiopian highlands will not descend to the plains for any length of time for fear of malaria.[1] Tsetse-infested belts further limit travel.

[1] E. E. Evans-Pritchard, *The Political Systems of the Anuak of the Anglo-Egyptian Sudan* (1940), pp. 7, 12.

Differentiation of environment, however, when it does not involve violent differences in temperature and disease, tends towards wider relations, for the differentiated areas supply complementary products. Gluckman has shown that the relatively wide communications of the Lozi were determined by differences in environment and production, particularly the difference between the flood plain and the bush country on its margins. People living in the flood plain lacked firewood and other products of the bush; those living in the bush lacked fish and other products of the plain:[1] thus trade between them developed. Evans-Pritchard has shown also how scarcity of water extended interdependence among the Nuer.[2] But density of population, be it noted, is not necessarily correlated with largeness of scale.[3] Nyakyusa society was smaller in scale than either Ngonde or Bemba society, yet the Nyakyusa are over 80 to the square mile,[4] while the men of Ngonde are under 15,[5] and the Bemba are never more than 3·9.[6]

As societies increase in scale the relative influence of the material environment diminishes, for control of it increases. Climatic variations matter less when men are provided with clothes and refrigerators and lorries, and the causation of disease is understood, than when their techniques and science are rudimentary. This, as we shall see, is one among a number of other social characteristics correlated with difference in scale. It is already evident that many of the changes taking place in Central Africa are correlated with

[1] Max Gluckman, *Economy of the Central Rotse Plain*, Rhodes-Livingstone Papers No. 7 (1941), *passim*.
[2] E. E. Evans-Pritchard, *The Nuer*, pp. 118–19.
[3] Cf. M. Fortes and E. E. Evans-Pritchard (editors), *African Political Systems*, pp. 7–8.
[4] Godfrey Wilson, *The Land Rights of Individuals among the Nyakyusa*, Rhodes-Livingstone Papers No. 1 (1938), p. 6.
[5] Godfrey Wilson, *The Constitution of Ngonde*, p. 7.
[6] Audrey Richards, *Land, Labour and Diet*, p. 18.

the change in scale; but their necessary connections, and the full implication of change in scale, cannot be described until we have analysed society more closely.

Societies, groups and individuals which are wide scale in their relations, and which exhibit the correlated social characteristics, we call civilized; those which are small scale in their relations, and exhibit the correlated social characteristics, we call primitive.

CHAPTER III

SOCIAL ELEMENTS

(a) CULTURE AND STRUCTURE

SOCIETY is, for sociology, the nexus of relations in which categories and groups of people are involved with one another. A category is a set of people whose position in society is similar, but who never join together and behave as a group. The uniqueness of the individual and his relations lies beyond the scope of sociology, which concerns itself only with general characteristics—that is, with the position and relations of categories and groups. Relations in society have a positive or cultural content and a negative or structural form. Positively, categories and groups of people enter into and continue in relations because of what they find in them; because the relations have for them some intrinsic value, some utility, some significance, and so on. Negatively, it is only by constantly checking one another's behaviour, by exerting mutual social pressure to limit each other's activities, that they can continue in relation. Relations are not possible without law, logic and convention.

As we have seen, relations vary in intensity; that is, in the degree of their direct realization. Some relations have, for the same categories and groups of people, more positive content, and involve more mutual limitation, than others. The same relations may have more positive content and involve more mutual limitation for some categories and groups of people than others.

Relations have three aspects: practical, intellectual, and emotional; and the positive content found in them is nothing less than the world. The world that is found has two aspects: first that of material existence, and second that of ultimate or religious reality. In practical relations with one another men both exploit the material (i.e. economic) resources of the world, and find in it a religious (i.e. moral) value; in intellectual relations they both investigate the material (i.e. scientific) facts of the world, and find in it a religious (i.e. dogmatic) significance; in emotional relations they both engage in material (i.e. technical) manipulation of the world, and find in it religious (i.e. aesthetic) qualities. The world that they thus find and deal with includes, but is also more than, the relations in which they find it. Human relations are themselves an economic resource, a scientific fact, a material for technical manipulation, but they are not the only ones; other resources, facts and materials are found in them. They themselves have value, significance and beauty, but so have other relations found in them.

This finding and dealing with the world, which is the positive content of human relations, we call collectively, culture, and severally, social activities. To realize a relation directly is, in the first place, to be joined in it by positive social activities. Minor nexuses of activity within community we call, if predominantly practical, *institutions*, if predominantly intellectual, *topics*; if predominantly emotional, *modes*.

Social activities involve both broad uniformities and detailed diversities of culture. Neither uniformity nor diversity by itself can provide any positive inducement to human beings to enter into or remain in relations with one another. It is complementary diversities, i.e. detailed diversities of culture within broad uniformities, that alone give rise to social activities. No category of business men could find anything useful to exchange with one another whose use of economic resources was either utterly different from or identical with its own, but only with one whose use of resources was differently specialized within a broadly similar economy. Trade between primitive and civilized groups is often small in volume at first because neither has much to offer that the other group wants.[1] Their requirements are too different. On the other hand, there was little trade between neighbouring Nyakyusa chiefdoms because they produced very much the same goods.

No category of theologians could find anything worth discussing with another whose dogmatic assumptions were either utterly different from or identical with its own, but only with one whose assumptions were, for it, intrinsically significant variations within a common metaphysic. How often is it said: 'I cannot argue with him; we proceed from totally different assumptions.' It is equally true that if people's ideas are very similar the only interest their conversation can hold is agreement in the contradiction of some other opinion.

No category of musicians could find it worth listening to another whose interpretation was utterly different from or identical with its own, but only to one whose interpretation was, for it, an intrinsically beautiful variation within a common art. It is in the individuality of an artistic creation that its attraction lies, but if taste be too dissimilar it is incompatible.

The distinction of categories and groups within society is thus in part positive or cultural. Each has its own diversity, peculiar to itself, which, within the broad uniformities of the society complements those of the others. The religious diversities of categories and groups we call *variations*; the material diversities *specialized functions*. When we are attending to the cultural distinctions of groups we speak of them as *associations*. Every group within society is,

[1] Cf. S. H. Frankel, *Capital Investment in Africa*, pp. 10–11.

in one aspect, an association. Although an association which has a territorial basis (e.g. a State) may coincide with a community, it is nevertheless to be distinguished from it.[1] The community is an area and period of common life of greater or less intensity: the association is a group with specialized functions or religious variations.

Within associations smaller associations are sometimes, and different cultural categories are always, distinguished. The religious variation and/or specialized function that distinguishes the larger association within the community is, for the smaller associations and categories within it, a broad uniformity, within which their own more detailed variations and specializations are further distinguished. For example, the British Medical Association is distinguished by its specialized function; but its specialization— the practice of medicine—is a uniformity for the surgeons, physicians and psychiatrists who specialize within it. The Royal College of Surgeons is, in turn, distinguished by its specialized function, but its specialization is again a uniformity for its Fellows who may specialize in particular fields of surgery. Thus the maintenance of the uniformity of a group is, at the same time, the maintenance of diversity between it and other groups.

The positive content of human relations in community can only be realized if the different categories and groups conform, in their diverse activities, to the uniformities that make them complementary, and thereby maintain their diversity. That they should press on one another to do so, when any eccentricity is attempted, is a structural necessity; for unless eccentricities were checked any nexus of human relations would quickly dissolve in anarchy.

[1] Cf. R. M. MacIver, *Community. The Modern State.*

(b) Social Structure

Social structure is the systematic form of limitation by which eccentricities are checked and complementary diversities are preserved: it is the inherent, negative condition of human relations. Its only, though sufficient, reason for existence is to make possible the realization of their positive content. In itself it is an empty form; it has neither value nor utility, significance nor informativeness, beauty nor technical serviceability. Being inherent in the relation it is something that categories and groups impose on one another; only they can do so, and only by its imposition can their relations be maintained. Social structure is the application of *social pressure*. It operates, in the practical aspect, as legal pressure maintaining the legal structure or organization of relations; in the intellectual aspect it operates as logical pressure maintaining the logical structure or system of relations; in the emotional aspect it operates as conventional pressure maintaining the conventional structure or pattern of relations. Law can only be observed in operation, that is, in the application of pressure against the law breakers. For the sociologist there is no law which is never broken. The same is true of logic and convention.

Social structure is a form of limitation; a form of order, coherence and harmony. By its very nature it can only check behaviour that flouts the accepted uniformities of the society concerned. Apart from this it leaves their behaviour free. Freedom from social pressure we call *autonomy*. Every category and group in society has autonomy within the structural limits set for it by the uniformities involved. This autonomy is secured by limitation: the limitation of A is at the same time the autonomy of B. Thus structure maintains, as well as limiting, freedom.

Social structure necessarily involves leadership and sub-ordination, i.e. inequalities of status. Uniformities can only be pressed by some categories and groups of people on others, i.e. some must have the capacity to co-ordinate the activities of others; and this capacity is leadership. Culturally the position of categories and groups in relation to one another is defined by their peculiar diversities within the nexus of social activities; structurally it is defined by their status within the inevitable nexus of leadership and subordination. Practical leadership we call *power*, intellectual leadership *intellectual authority*, and conventional leadership *prestige*. The legal organization is maintained by the exercise of power, the logical system by that of intellectual authority, conventional patterns by that of prestige.

The content of relative status varies with the content of relations. In primarily moral relations power is a matter of social worth, in primarily economic relations of wealth; in primarily dogmatic relations intellectual authority is a matter of wisdom, in primarily scientific relations of knowledge; in primarily aesthetic relations prestige is a matter of beauty, in primarily technical relations of skill.

Inequalities of status are necessarily limited, because they are relative to one another. Everyone has some power, some intellectual authority and some prestige. A's rights are B's obligations, and the capacity of different categories and groups to exert social pressure in different situations dovetail in together. Autonomy—freedom from social pressure—is the negative aspect of leadership—the capacity to exert social pressure.

Social pressure operates by causing loss of relative social status to the category or group which fails to co-operate or communicate in the approved form. It is the inevitable diminution of status in which an eccentric category or group is involved by its eccentricity. Its effectiveness is derived from, or rather is part of, the status of those who exert it. The higher the status of a category or group the greater the pressure it exerts. The disapproval of kings is very embarrassing; of beggars only slightly so. Economic pressure derives its force from the wealth of those who apply it. If a Nyakyusa boy is lazy about hoeing, his father will be slow to give him marriage cattle: the effectiveness of the sanction depends upon the possession of cattle by the father. If the boy is very ill-behaved his father may curse him; but the effectiveness of the curse is dependent upon the social worth of the father. If the father is in the wrong the curse will not operate: similarly, scientific arguments derive their cogency from the knowledge of those who use them, dogmatic arguments from their wisdom.

Social structure is both sectional and general. Every group in a community has its own uniformity which must be maintained by social pressure, and which, in consequence, involves internal leadership and subordination. Every group must itself conform to a wider uniformity; that is, it is involved in a general nexus of leadership and subordination. In the practical aspect confusion arises from the accepted verbal distinction between the organization of larger and smaller groups. The limitations maintained by states, or associations of states, are called laws: those maintained by smaller groups (as schools or trade unions) are called rules. We could only accept this distinction if parallel distinctions were accepted in the intellectual and emotional fields; if we ceased to speak of a particular science as 'having its own logic', or of the 'conventions' of contract bridge, and substituted new terms for the logic and conventions of smaller groups. Failing this we must use law o include sectional as well as general organization.

If law be used for sectional as well as for general limitation a distinction commonly made between legal pressure on the one hand, and economic and moral pressure on the other, disappears. 'Economic' and 'moral' pressure are commonly used for sectional pressure, such as is exercised by an employer against an incompetent workman, or by neighbours against a woman neglecting her children. Dismissal of a workman, and disapproval of neighbours, we include under legal pressure. Moreover, the legal pressure exerted by a state is always both economic and moral in content. Fines imposed by courts are an economic sanction, and so is their frequent alternative, imprisonment; while both are accompanied by public disapproval and derive part of their terror from that fact. The death penalty is simply the greatest economic and moral loss it is possible to impose. Similarly, as Italy insisted in 1936, there is no difference in principle between economic and military sanctions imposed by one state on another.

Law is an inherent necessity of practical co-operation, which cannot continue unless conflict is restrained. Law limits the forms of co-operation between people so as to make co-operation possible. Conflict arises in one relation, above all, when other relations are incompatible with it. If A's practical relation to B is incompatible with his relation to C, then conflict must arise in one or other, or in both, the relations. Thus each particular form of co-operation must so be limited as to be compatible with other forms; and law is, at once, the limitation and the organization of co-operation.

It is usual to distinguish between organization, or administration, on the one hand, and the making and enforcing of laws on the other; but organization is simply the making and enforcing of detailed or sectional laws to avoid detailed, sectional conflicts. A modern state makes laws of general application to all fields of action, and enforces them. It also organizes, or administers, certain of these fields in detail, leaving other fields to be administered by other authorities: domestic, local, economic and religious. To the sociologist an administrative rule is sectional law.

Law is thus an organized series of laws, or rules—some more general, some more detailed, some traditional, some of recent invention—that are actively enforced in a given society. In studying law it is the rule as enforced, not the rule as verbally formulated, that interests us. People may pay lip service to a rule that they do not in fact obey, and that no one enforces on them: such a 'rule' is no law at all.

Laws are enforced by the application of pressure (either economic or moral, or, usually, both at once) on those who break them. The pressure compels the lawbreaker either to conform or, through the process of social separation (*vide infra*, pp. 60–1), to seek other relations in which his behaviour will be legal. Such other relations often exist, for the diversity of categories and groups within society involves detailed differences between the sectional laws that apply to them. General laws cannot be avoided, sectional laws sometimes can through a change of group. Behaviour, for instance, that is against the rules of an explosives' factory and that leads there to continual fines and reprimands, may be unpenalized on a farm.

The enforcement of law is possible because those who enforce it have power over those who break it: the group, or its representatives, enforce law on the individual; those of higher status on those of lower.

Logic, since Descartes, has usually been conceived solely as the avoidance of conceptual contradiction, but this is to miss its full nature. Primarily logic is the avoidance of contradiction between people, and hence of conceptual contradiction. Logic is the inherent necessity of intellectual communication, which cannot continue unless contradiction is restrained. It enables people to communicate with one another by limiting the conceptual forms in which they do so. It is only by using conceptual forms in a carefully limited, i.e. defined or qualified, sense that people can avoid contradicting one another in using them. By conceptual forms we mean not only words and mathematical symbols, but, also and above all, complete statements.

In the case of words (and mathematical symbols) it is obvious that, unless people use the same words (or symbols) in the same limited sense, they will inevitably be involved in contradiction whenever they try to communicate with one another. They must agree on the definition of the words they use. Similarly, in the case of statements, people must agree about their qualifications, i.e. about the limitations of the truth they convey. Few statements are true without qualification,[1] and unless people agree what the qualifications of a particular statement are they will inevitably contradict one another in making it. The land-tenure discussion that is reproduced below is an example of this.

Moreover, it would seem that the definitions of words and the qualifications of statements must be generally agreed on in a given society if contradiction is to be avoided. If one group uses words in one sense, and another in another, if one makes a statement with one set of qualifications implied, and another makes it with another set implied, then contradiction will arise whenever members of the two groups use these words or make this statement to each other. This general agreement about definitions and qualifications, however, is not quite absolute in any

---

[1] There are some statements which, once the words have been defined, are generally accepted as true without qualification: e.g. 'All men are mortal.' Most statements, however, are not of this kind.

society. In the case of the commoner words and statements it must be approximately absolute, or contradictions could not be avoided; for these words and statements are always being employed in all relations. But in the case of less common words and statements it is possible for the diverse categories and groups of the society to use them in slightly different senses and with slightly different qualifications, without destroying the logical structure. It is possible because, and in so far as, the different categories and groups have relatively little to do with one another. When members of two groups meet, contradiction can be avoided by confining communication to the words and statements on whose limitations they agree, and avoiding those on which they disagree. Protestants and Catholics, for instance, can discuss the weather and the virtues of Mr Churchill, but avoid discussing the nature of the Church. In short, the sectional logic of different categories and groups need not be identical and never is wholly identical; but there is always a general logic in any society, consisting of common words and statements on whose definitions and qualifications everyone is normally agreed.

We recall a discussion on land-tenure, among the Nyakyusa, over a pot of beer. We asked what would happen to a man's house-site if, after leaving it voluntarily, he returned to find it reallotted to another man. Two contradictory answers were given: one side said he would be given it back and the newcomer evicted, the other side said that he could not get it back and would be given another site instead. We then sat back while the contradiction was resolved by the disputants. Various qualifications were made which limited the application of the two contradictory statements to different situations until both sides were agreed: in some cases he would get his site back, in others not. This was a piece of living logic. The subject of discussion may be anything, but its logical form is always the same: contradiction is resolved by the definition of words and the qualification of statements. The definition of words and the qualification of statements is, at the same time, the systematic relation to other words and statements. Logic is both the limitation and the systematizing of words and statements in order to avoid contradiction.

Logic, like law and convention, is maintained by social pressure. Accepted definitions and qualifications are imposed on those who flout them by the weight of intellectual authority; the group or its representative impose them on the individual, those of higher status on those of lower. In the land-tenure example quoted, a leading part in the discussion was taken by a great-commoner (village headman) who was an expert on the subject of land-tenure; his opinion carried more weight than that of the others, and he took the chief part in formulating the qualifications that led to final agreement. Some stood out against his qualifications for a time, but gave in when they saw that the majority was with him.

The pressure exercised by intellectual authority consists sometimes of scientific facts and connections, sometimes of dogmatic opinions, which are generally accepted in the society or the group concerned, and with which they bombard the illogical person. The pressure compels him either to conform in his definitions and qualifications to the accepted logic, or, through the process of social separation, to seek other relations in which his own will prove acceptable. The existence of sectional variety in logic means that such other relations may at times be available; the Protestant may become a Catholic, or vice versa.

Convention, again, is an inherent necessity of emotional relations, which cannot continue unless disharmonies of emotional expression are restrained. Convention limits the forms of expression so as to make emotional relations possible. Disharmonies arise in one relation, above all, when other relations are expressly incompatible with it: if A's emotional relation to his wife B is expressly incompatible with his relation to her father C, then disharmonies of expression are bound to arise in one or the other, or in both relations. He may be courteous and affectionate to her and rude to her father, for instance; but then the rudeness to her father will be felt by her as a personal discourtesy, and the express harmony of their relations will be broken. It is necessary that the conventional limits of expression in one relation should be themselves harmonious with those in all other relations, in any given society, if emotional relations are to continue. Convention is at once the limitation and the harmonizing of emotional expressions.

Convention, be it noted, limits expression only, not feeling. In the instance given above the husband may continue to hate his wife's father in his heart; but, provided he is expressly courteous to him, harmony is none the less preserved.

Convention, then, is a harmonious series of conventions that are, in a given society, emotionally obligatory. Their obligatory nature is maintained by the pressure of shame on those who break them. Shame compels the unconventional either to conform or, through the process of social separation, to seek other relations in which his behaviour will be accepted as conventional. Such other relations are often present, for the general harmony of the conventions of a given society does not exclude diversity of convention between different groups within it. Wherever two groups such as 'Bohemians' and 'Puritans' have relatively little to do with one another, there it is possible for them to maintain some different conventions without breaking the general social harmony.

People feel shame when involved in disharmony with those who have prestige in their eyes, a prestige which, whether because of numbers or status, is higher than their own. An individual involved in disharmony with a group or with its representatives, a man of lower status involved in disharmony with one of higher, feels ashamed.

Shame is the felt pressure of convention on the unconventional person; its content may be either aesthetic or technical or both. In primarily aesthetic situations the behaviour of the unconventional is distasteful to his fellows and their expression of distaste shames him. In primarily technical situations it is unskilful, or clumsy, behaviour that is unconventional, i.e. shameful. The poor artist in a circle of better ones is ashamed of his bad taste; the poor executant playing before the virtuoso is ashamed of his lack of skill.

(c) SOCIAL CIRCULATION

Within all societies there is social circulation: that is, the members of the various categories and groups change, and leaders and subordinates change. External conditions necessitate social circulation—men die and are born, and the function and status of every man necessarily changes as he develops from infancy to old age. The way in which a man's position changes with his development varies from society to society, but the biological conditions which necessitate some change remain constant. Everywhere there is marriage and inheritance in one form or another.

Social circulation—the change of occupants of existing positions—is to be distinguished from social change, that is, change of the positions to be occupied in society. In the one case it is only the personnel which changes; in the other the social activities and relations of the various categories and groups in society change.[1]

Social circulation includes the splitting and reforming of groups that is constantly going on in societies. In Pondoland, for example, the local kinship group, the *umzi*, periodically split into two or more, a son or brother of the head of the original group moving away with his own immediate followers to build an *umzi* for himself.[2] But the constitution of the *umzi* in Pondo society was not thereby affected, for while some *imizi* were splitting others were increasing in size, as their sons grew up and married and begot children. Similarly, in BuNyakyusa, chiefdoms divided into two independent halves when the sons of the old chief and their followers reached maturity. At the same time very small chiefdoms were absorbed by larger neighbours. There is no evidence that the average size of chiefdoms changed appreciably. The population and territory occupied by them was expanding, and this expansion, coupled with the absorption of smaller chiefdoms, probably meant that the average size and density remained more or less constant and that, except where people of a different culture were absorbed, the system of relations was but a repetition of the system in the parent chiefdom.[3] Gluckman gives evidence of similar tribal fission and fusion, combined with territorial expansion, among the Zulu, before the development of 'kingdoms' began. 'Quarrels between and within tribes were part of the social system, but they led to no change in the organization of each tribe or the

[1] Cf. A. R. Radcliffe-Brown, 'On social structure', *Journal of the Royal Anthropological Institute*, Part 1, 1940, p. 4.
[2] Monica Hunter, *Reaction to Conquest*, 1936, p. 23.
[3] Cf. Godfrey Wilson, 'An introduction to Nyakyusa society', *Bantu Studies*, Sept. 1936. Our evidence on these points is incomplete.

congery of tribes.'[1] Similarly, in the historical moment, the range of tradition probably remained constant at ten or twelve generations. A more distant ancestor whose exploits were famous might be remembered, but as time passed the intervening generations were telescoped, and the hero was still represented as living but ten or twelve generations back.[2]

When, however, fission or fusion involves a diminution or an increase in scale (contemporary or historical), a fragmentation or an expansion of the existing society, then there is social change (*vide infra*, p. 135).

Besides the external reasons for social circulation there are specifically social reasons. These are of two kinds, positive and negative, i.e. cultural and structural. Men enter into new relations because these have a positive content for them, as in the case of youths marrying and setting up their own households; and because they are compelled to do so by social pressure—the girl who remains unmarried in a primitive society, for example, is derided. The negative reason for circulation is the wish to escape social pressure.

As we have already pointed out, people involved in opposition in one group often take advantage of the diversity which exists in every society to avoid social pressure, not by conformity to the sectional law, logic, and convention of the group concerned, but by moving to another group. To take an extreme example, a communist may escape from Germany to the U.S.S.R. and his beliefs which were heterodox in Germany are orthodox in the U.S.S.R. Less acute, but strictly comparable, is the case of the intellectual living among non-intellectuals with

[1] Max Gluckman, 'Analysis of a social situation in modern Zululand', *Bantu Studies*, June 1940, pp. 148–51.

[2] Cf. E. E. Evans-Pritchard, *The Nuer*, p. 108.

whom he has few interests in common, and who regard his passion for books or music as 'cranky'. He may change his associates for others having tastes similar to his own. Such change of group to avoid social pressure we call *social separation*. It includes also separation due to personal incompatibility, as divorce; for personal idiosyncrasies are among the diversities of society.

Social separation is only effective as a means of avoiding pressure when the eccentricity of the individual concerned in one group is not eccentric in another. The communist finds asylum because socialist states exist; the intellectual can pursue his taste unmocked by friends because intellectual groups exist; but the homicidal maniac is welcomed nowhere.

Social separation may or may not involve some loss of status to the individual separating, but always by separating he loses less status than he would were he to remain in his former group and refuse to conform. The refugee may be poor, but he suffers less than he would were he to remain in his own country.

(d) SCIENCE AND PHILOSOPHY

The distinction between the religious or metaphysical and the matter of fact aspects of culture is current in our society. We use it because without it we cannot analyse the facts. Our defence is empirical: its use makes the facts more intelligible. The general distinction between the religious and the matter of fact leads us to the more specific distinction, within the intellectual field, between philosophy and science.

In Western civilization science and philosophy are observably distinct, but not independent, elements of intellectual activity. Each includes and depends on the other.

Philosophy, the religious element, includes the discussion of fact, in so far as fact possesses religious relevance, but philosophy is not concerned with the detailed analysis of fact. Its special concern is with the truth and falsehood of the various dogmas in the light of which men find their lives significant. Science, the material element, includes the analysis of religion, and so of philosophy, in so far as philosophy is objective, that is, fact; but science is not concerned with the truth or falsehood of philosophy. Its special concern is with the detailed nature of fact, its material determinants and material implication. The facts with which science deals are not particular realities, i.e. nations, persons, things or events as such; but only their various material characteristics: physical, organic, psychological, social. It is not only in its totality, but also in its particularity, that reality transcends our scientific analysis. No particular event, for instance, is wholly dealt with by any modern science, but only some material characteristics of it. Nor do all the sciences together give a complete account of any event; for not only is it true that the mere addition of a physical to a biological, and of both to a psychological and sociological account, does not explain the unity of these different characteristics in a single event; but there is also, in the character of every event, a certain margin of indeterminism unaccounted for. As with events, so with nations, persons and things—their integral character escapes the nets of current science.

It is an axiom of current science that the material characteristics of reality, which characteristics we call 'facts', are linked in universal systems of necessary connection which it is the scientist's business to explore. The general form of our scientific law is as follows: any particular relation with certain material characteristics must also have, wherever and whenever it exists, certain other material characteristics. No necessary connection between particular realities as such is ever disclosed. The facts of current science are not integral realities but systems of necessary connection, in which, through their material characteristics, realities are involved.

The assertion that particular realities do exist, e.g. that particular events have actually occurred, is the starting place both of the sciences and of philosophy; but, whereas science concentrates, in making such an assertion, on describing those material characteristics of the events with which it is specifically concerned, philosophy concentrates on describing the total (or integral or intrinsic) character of the events themselves. Their total character includes their material characteristics, but goes beyond them.

Current philosophy also links particular realities together in universal and logically coherent systems, but in a different way. Instead of linking them indirectly and partially through their various material characteristics, it links them directly and absolutely, through their intrinsic character. It is able to do this because, and only because, it makes dogmatic assumptions about the intrinsic character of reality as a whole, of which the intrinsic character of each particular reality is taken as a disclosure. It is this linking of particular realities, in their intrinsic character, to one another and to reality as a whole that gives them significance.

Philosophy is thus concerned with the explanation of events, and of other particular realities, in dogmatic, that is, religious terms. Science is concerned with the analysis of their necessary factual connections. The word *explanation* is sometimes used of the analysis of science, but as this use annoys the philosophers[1] and leads to confusion, we are sedulous to avoid it.

[1] Cf. R. F. A. Hoernlé, 'Philosophers and anthropologists', *Bantu Studies*, Dec. 1940 (Vol. xiv, No. 4).

The method of current scientific analysis is empirical, not dogmatic. About reality as a whole it makes only a certain minimum of axiomatic assumptions—such as that the material characteristics of reality are everywhere comparable. In its description of particular realities it confines itself to observable material characteristics, and strives to beg as few questions as possible about intrinsic character and meaning. Finally, and most important, it proves the connections of fact, which logical argument suggests to it, by careful and repeated comparative observation.

To the observable connections of fact in various particular cases current science strives to give a universal form. It strives to link the fall of an apple to earth with all other possible movements of physical objects in relation to one another, by laying bare the general principles that govern them. It strives likewise to link the absorption of a primitive society into a world civilization with all other possible historical movements, by laying bare the general principles or laws that govern them. These laws can only be demonstrated by comparative observation in widely differing situations. No amount of research into the fall of apples, plums and fir-cones would have sufficed to prove Newton's law of gravity; to do that it was necessary to observe also the movements of the solar system. So any historical laws that we and our colleagues may suggest as a result of research into the movements of detribalization, will remain hypothetical until tested out by historians in other situations.

Although current scientific laws are universal in form they remain tentative or hypothetical. We may prove that they govern all movement known to-day; but to-morrow fresh observation, by more refined methods, may necessitate their modification; as has already happened with the law of gravity. It often happens, moreover, in the process of discovery, that rival hypotheses are in the field together. One set of facts seems to suggest one law, another, another; the two hypotheses are momentarily irreconcilable, and neither is adequate to cover all the facts; but in the end a modification of one or the other is bound to prevail and be generally accepted.

In some sciences the necessary comparative observation of fact usually takes the form of controlled experiment. In others (such as astronomy, geology, archaeology, and both animal and human sociology) experiment is rarely possible, but they are none the less tied to comparative observation for their proof of factual connections.

The method of current philosophy is dogmatic or *a priori*. About reality as a whole it makes initial assumptions which are taken as fundamental, i.e. unquestioned. *Cogito ergo sum* and *God so loved the world* are examples of such initial assumptions. From these assumptions it deduces the meaning of the particular realities of life; or, to put the fact in another way, by making these assumptions it illuminates their intrinsic character.[1] The assumptions of philosophy are sometimes said to be 'self-evident'; but, as they differ from one school of philosophy to the next, it is clear that this can only mean that there is no unquestionable outside evidence for them. There cannot be: their truth or falsehood is intrinsic. They cannot be proved or disproved; they can only be taken or left.

The connections asserted by philosophy to obtain between particular realities as such are, then, simply an extension of its initial assumptions; they also are integral or absolute in character, and they stand or fall with them;

---

[1] For example, 'We cannot ascertain the character of God by induction from what he has done and is doing in nature and history. But when we have found it in Jesus Christ we can begin to trace it there also': W. Temple, *Readings in St John's Gospel*, Series 1, p. 155.

they cannot be fully substantiated by any empirical observation, for they are assertions not of material fact, but of reality and meaning.

The philosopher normally takes for granted the proven connections of fact in which science deals; and he must do so. A 'purely metaphysical' statement without objective reference would be immaterial; and no such statement is ever made. The scientist, likewise, normally takes for granted, in the form of axioms, certain generally accepted dogmas; and he must do so. A 'purely scientific' statement without dogmatic implications would be insignificant, and no such statement is ever made. The autonomy of science, like that of philosophy, is relative, not absolute. Sometimes, indeed, an axiom which science needs is not, as a dogma, generally accepted; and then a Huxley may be forced outside his field into metaphysical argument, or a bishop outside his into denial of 'proven fact'.

It is often not realized by scientists that their axioms are not primarily scientific but dogmatic assumptions. The empirical success of the sciences which proceed from these assumptions undoubtedly tends to confirm, though it cannot prove, their philosophical truth; but their making is a precondition and determinant of that success. In these axioms modern science and modern philosophy meet and determine each other.

It is a necessary condition of Western science that practically all schools of Western philosophy—Catholic, Protestant, Materialist and Humanist—now include these axioms as dogmas in their systems. If they did not, then scientists could not take them for granted as they do, and the whole form of modern science would be changed. Scientists can only get their facts and laws accepted by those who already accept their axioms. If many people did not, then the scientists would either have to change their axioms (and so engage in a different kind of science) or else spend time in waging metaphysical war. If racial philosophy, for instance, were much to increase its hold on modern thought,[1] then social scientists would find themselves in this dilemma; for that particular philosophy denies the axioms of current social science, by denying the comparability of human groups.

It is a no less necessary condition of philosophy that its objective reference should be taken as scientifically valid. No philosopher can get much of a hearing if the majority of his hearers deny the facts in which he claims to find a meaning. Were our present social science less embryonic, racial philosophy could not have established itself, for to accept the facts and laws of a science is necessarily to accept its axioms within one's metaphysical system.

The distinction between science and philosophy, then, is only relative. Each determines the other. In our common speech the two are inextricably mingled. Assertions of fact and dogma follow and coalesce with each other without clear distinction.

Some readers may have been puzzled by the apparent paradox of first distinguishing science, the matter-of-fact activity, from philosophy, the religious activity, and then going on to say that philosophy, no less than science, is itself a matter of fact. Once the relative nature of the distinction is grasped, however, the paradox disappears. Philosophy, like science, is observable in human discussion, its particular manifestations therein can be dated, located and objectively described; their social determinants and implications can be traced with certainty; they are social facts, material characteristics of human social behaviour subject to historical laws. To say this, however, is not to

---

[1] Its hold is not confined to Germany. Cf. L. Hogben, *Dangerous Thoughts*, pp. 44–52.

dissolve philosophy away. It has its own autonomy no less, if no more, than science.

If it be asked how a dogma can be an observable fact—how we can know what people really believe—we reply that while science has no certain knowledge of particular cases as such, the beliefs common to a whole group of persons can be observed, in an intelligible form, constantly manifesting themselves in speech and writing. These are indisputable facts, though particular individuals may lie.

Exception may also be taken to our inclusion of philosophy in the religious aspect of behaviour, and our consequent identification of critical with religious argument. 'Philosophy', says Macmurray, 'is largely concerned with the criticism and examination of prejudice.'[1] And some readers no doubt would change his 'largely' into 'exclusively'. Philosophy, they would argue, is concerned with the destruction, not with the affirmation, of religious prejudice or dogma. Such an objection proceeds from too narrow a conception of what a dogma is. A dogma is not necessarily theistic, still less Christian, in content; it is an affirmation of a certain integral character resident both in events, things, persons and peoples, and in reality as a whole. It is observable that every philosophy is the elaboration, it may be diffidently undertaken, of certain dogmas; and that the critical force which enables the philosopher to call in question other people's dogmas is directly derived from his own. There are philosophers who try to maintain a consistent scepticism; but this attempt itself rests on the dogmatic assumption that reality is not, properly speaking, knowable. Materialists also maintain that they have no religious beliefs, but their very assertion that events are determined solely by material connections is in itself a

[1] John Macmurray, *The Boundaries of Science*, p. 25.

dogma, strictly comparable to the dogma that they are not thus solely determined.

Philosophy is the intellectual element of religion and includes theology. The distinction sometimes made in our civilization between 'theologians' and 'philosophers' points not to any difference in the type of their activity, but only to a difference in the dogmas they affirm.

In applying the distinction between science (concern with fact) and philosophy (concern with dogma) to primitive culture we meet an apparent difficulty. The distinction is not at all clearly made by the primitives themselves. In their speech the two are inextricably mingled. When a Nyakyusa tells us that a child has died of witchcraft, we split his statement up, and say that the first part of it asserts a fact—the occurrence of an event with certain material characteristics—the second the intrinsic character or dogmatic meaning which he finds in it. But he does not say this himself. Since we are setting out to be empirical scientists, dealing only with observable fact, and in primitive societies the general distinction between fact and dogma is not directly observable, how are we justified in making it?

Our first answer as scientists is a plea of necessity. For us this distinction is not mere fact, though it is an observable fact in our culture; for us it is also an axiom, a category of scientific thought, without which we cannot speak intelligibly, of primitive or any other cultures. If we denied it, along with other general distinctions (such as that between action, concept and expression) which we import in the same way into primitive cultures, then we cannot either describe or analyse them clearly.

Our second answer is that only on the assumption that all societies, whether primitive or civilized, are comparable, is a science of sociology possible. This assumption is

axiomatic, and it involves the corollary that every fact of
any one society is somehow paralleled in all others. The
general distinction between fact and dogma is a given fact
in our own society; it must therefore be paralleled in all
others. And we find, as Malinowski and others have
repeatedly pointed out,[1] that although the primitives make
no such general distinction, they do make various particular
distinctions which are comparable.

Now the universal logical form of our philosophy and
science is commonly taken as their essential characteristic,
and it is therefore denied that the primitives have either.
Evans-Pritchard, for instance, denies that the Azande have
a science,[2] partly on the ground that their 'common-sense
notions', which he distinguishes from their 'mystical
notions', are not systematic and logical. The universal
logical form of our modern thought is a part of the structure
of a world-wide society: it is impossible that small-scale
societies should ever manifest it. But, we maintain, the
essential mark of science is empiricism,[3] of philosophy,
dogmatic assumption, and these are found both in primitive
and civilized societies. They may, or may not, be expressed

---

[1] B. Malinowski, *Coral Gardens and Their Magic*, Vol. I, pp. 75–7; *Argonauts
of the Western Pacific*, pp. 302–3, 396, 414, 420–1; Essay on 'Magic, science
and religion', in *Science, Religion and Reality*, edited J. Needham.

[2] E. E. Evans-Pritchard, *Witchcraft, Oracles and Magic among the Azande*,
p. 12.

[3] Both Evans-Pritchard (*op. cit.* p. 12) and Raymond Firth (*Human Types*,
p. 150) distinguish primitive 'common-sense notions' or 'rational principles' (Firth) from primitive religious dogmas, by reference to the content
of our own science. Anything which our present science can accept is
empirical, everything else is religious. This is surely erroneous. Much of
Newton's physics has been superseded, but it is not, therefore, proved
unscientific. The man who says his child has died of witchcraft may be
mistaken in fact, as well as 'misguided' in dogma: his child may be in a
coma. The essence of science is its empirical method, its appeal to an
observation which is relatively free, even if only for a moment, from dogmatic
certainty. Correctness of observation and of the resulting generalizations,
is not essential.

in universal form. As we shall see, however, in the succeeding chapter, universality diminishes the scope of magic and increases that of science.

Magical dogma dominates primitive thought, and magic limits the development of science; nevertheless, primitives do observe factual connections, and this observation enters into all their activities. Nyakyusa doctors told us that they experimented with medicines, seeking the most effective, and Mr and Mrs Krige report similar experiments among the Lovedu.[1] The intelligent adaptation of traditional agricultural systems to environment is clearly demonstrated in the report of the Ecological Survey of Northern Rhodesia.[2] Evans-Pritchard himself proves the coexistence of empirical and *a priori* methods among the Azande with an abundance of evidence,[3] the conclusiveness of which is unaffected by his reluctance to apply to the first the label 'scientific'. Which method is dominant, on any particular occasion, depends upon the success or failure of empirical methods, and upon the gravity of the occasion. Malinowski has constantly insisted that magic is resorted to when science fails.[4] Evans-Pritchard shows that the Azande, when things are going well with them, are empirical, but when disaster comes they at once refer to religious dogma.[5] The Pondo also attribute slight illness to natural causes such as bad food, or too much beer, or infection, but serious illness which does not yield to treatment is always attributed to religious causes.[6] It is not, however, situations of disaster alone which call forth religious explanation from primi-

[1] Verbal communication.
[2] Trapnell and Clothier, *op. cit.* pp. 23-58; cf. E. J. and J. D. Krige, *The Realm of a Rain Queen*, 1943, Chap. III.
[3] Evans-Pritchard, *op. cit.* pp. 65-80.
[4] B. Malinowski, *Argonauts*, pp. 395-6; *Coral Gardens*, Vol. I, p. 444.
[5] Evans-Pritchard, *op. cit.* pp. 63-83.
[6] Hunter, *op. cit.* pp. 272-5.

tives. All situations of emotional tension do so.[1] The mass of dogma that clusters round the sexual act is an obvious example.

A final difficulty remains. We have already noted that the prevalence of Christian dogma in our society tends to too narrow a concept of what a dogma is. The Christian God is an invisibly transcendent deity, whose reality is held to lie 'beyond', as well as in, the particular realities of everyday life; and it is, in consequence, often supposed that every religious dogma has a transcendent reference. This is not so, as a moment's consideration of the various purely immanent philosophies of modern thought (such as dialectic materialism) will show. A dogma interprets everyday realities, it may be by reference to a partly transcendent, or it may be by reference to a purely immanent, reality. We suggest that this misconception of the nature of dogma is largely responsible for the traditional radical distinction between *religion* and *magic* which we are abandoning in this book. Magic for us, though it may not postulate any transcendent reality, is an integral part of primitive religion.

In most primitive societies some of the accepted dogmas are theistic. They refer to supposed supernatural (i.e. transcendent) beings—ancestral spirits, gods and demons. Other dogmas commonly found refer to the supposed power of witchcraft—a power belonging to certain human beings but operating beyond (i.e. transcending) the range of everyday observation.[2] Magical dogma, on the other hand, is not transcendental. It is the very material particularity of events which is held to be significant. The presence of particular people, of particular social status, at

---

[1] Cf. Radcliffe-Brown, *The Andaman Islanders*, p. 263; Malinowski, *Argonauts*, pp. 392–6.

[2] We use the illuminating distinction between witchcraft and sorcery made by Evans-Pritchard, *op. cit.* p. 21 *et passim*.

a particular place and time, together with the use of particular words and materials in a particular manner, is held to be inherently magical. Such an assertion is as dogmatic as the Nicene Creed; for it is an assertion of intrinsic character and meaning. It is not cautious induction from observable connection of fact; it is an *a priori* assumption about reality.

Dogmas of theism and witchcraft on the one hand, and of magic on the other, are not mutually exclusive. Magical dogma asserts that the material characteristics of a particular reality are essential to its intrinsic character. It does not necessarily assert that no partly transcendent reality is also disclosed in it. A sickness which is held to be sent by the ancestors is no less magically conceived because of its theistic reference. It is magically conceived because it asserts that the ancestors have directly determined the material facts, as well as the intrinsic character of the event. In the same way a ritual killing to propitiate the ancestors is magically conceived when its specific material circumstances are regarded as essential to its intrinsic character, and so to its success.

(e) ECONOMICS AND MORALITY

In the practical field of human behaviour the distinction between the matter of fact and the religious aspects also applies. Here it leads us to distinguish the economic element of efficiency from the moral element of value. All co-operative actions must be both efficient in their use of material resources—time, energy, tools, material environment, and objective social relations—and have moral value for the people concerned. This distinction again is relative.

In Western civilization the relative autonomy of these two elements of action is clear. In 'business hours' millions of people normally take for granted the value of what they are doing, and concentrate on its efficient execution. Sometimes—as in an act of worship, or in the enjoyment of a holiday—they take the means momentarily for granted, and attend mainly to ends. But at other times—as in ordinary domestic life for instance—the two elements are so intermingled that they can only be held apart by an effort of thought. Their distinction and their unity is exactly parallel to that of science and philosophy, of which they are the practical correlates.

Efficient execution is no more the whole of an act than fact is the whole of an event. Efficient execution is the mastery of the act's material implications; it is the economical use of material resources. The resources available are always limited; if they are wasted, i.e. if more are used for a particular act than is necessary, then other potentially practicable acts become impracticable. This limitation of resources is the material necessity that governs the practical field. It makes the avoidance of waste an inevitable element of every action. Within the same social field it links all actions, through their common need of resources, in a determinate manner.

Efficient execution involves scientific knowledge and technical skill. Action, concept and expression are not separable fields of human behaviour, and each involves the other. But economics, or efficient execution, is distinct both from science and from technique; it is the practical management of limited resources.

Efficient execution in itself is morally neutral, but it implies values to be realized. Unless the act were taken by the agents as somehow worth while no movement in its execution would be made. In predominantly economic activities men may concentrate on the avoidance of material waste, but they take therein certain values for granted.

Such given values govern all predominantly economic activity, and are strictly parallel to the axioms of science.

The morality of co-operative action is its supposed value or intrinsic goodness, as distinct from its use of material resources. Morality is manifest in action, and is to be distinguished from ethics,[1] which is the discussion of morals. Morals can be discussed either scientifically as a set of facts or philosophically as part of the integral meaning of events, but they *are* the performance of supposedly valuable actions. Since by morality we mean all the values people seek in action, the morality of Western civilization includes the accumulation of individual wealth and power, as well as the attempts to apply the Sermon on the Mount.

Social values can be observed in institutions. Professor Macmurray has argued that the human sciences cannot deal with value because they cannot observe intention.[2] His argument, however, only shows that it is impossible to be certain of the *particular* intention behind a *particular* action, and there we agree with him. But the sociologist is not concerned with particular intentions; he is concerned with the normal values, observably manifest in an intelligibly similar form in the behaviour of many individuals on many occasions.

All social values are related to the supposed character of the universe. For the communist, for example, action is good which manifests or tends towards the establishment of the classless society; for the Nazi action is good which manifests or tends towards German dominance; for the Christian action is good which manifests or tends towards the Kingdom of God; for the humanist action is good which makes for the happiness of majority; for the Nyakyusa action

---

[1] Cf. H. W. Fowler, *Modern English Usage.*
[2] John Macmurray, *op. cit.* pp. 142–3.

is good which makes for fertility. But to the communist the classless society is the inevitable outcome of the historical process; to the Nazi Germans are destined to dominate; to the Christian the Kingdom of God will be established; to the humanist the desire for happiness is 'natural' and can be fulfilled if men follow the laws of the universe as exposed in science; to the Nyakyusa fertility is the nature of things. Goodness, therefore, is acting in accordance with the supposed character of the universe, and values, though not necessarily transcendental, are always religious. The classless society, German domination, the Kingdom of God, the happiness of the majority, fertility, are, for those who believe in them, both the touchstone of value and the essential nature of reality.

It may be objected that since value is observed in action rather than in speech, the fact that the Christian Church does not manifest the Kingdom of God very clearly, nor the Communist Party the classless society, proves that the Kingdom and the classless society cannot be the real values of these organizations. But their failure to achieve their ends does not mean that they do not pursue them. If no one believed in the Kingdom of God or the classless society, neither the Christian Church nor the Communist Party would exist.

In applying the distinction between economics and morality to primitive societies we find, as we should expect, that it is not very clearly given in them; but that in particular situations a comparable distinction is observable.

(f) TECHNIQUE AND ART

In the emotional field of human behaviour our general distinction also applies. Here it leads us to distinguish the material element of technique, or craft, from the religious element of art. Any expression of emotion—and all human behaviour is, in one aspect, expressive—must be both a more or less successful piece of material manipulation and an expression of intrinsic quality.

In Western civilization the relative autonomy of these two elements is clear. Many craftsmen concentrate on the skilful handling of materials without directly attending to the intrinsic quality of the work on which they are engaged. This elaboration of skill is correlated, both as cause and effect, with the similar elaboration of science and economics. On the other hand, we have artists—painters, composers, poets, sculptors and others who attend mainly to the expression of intrinsic quality. They, though necessarily skilled, are not primarily concerned with technique. Their status as artists depends on the quality of what they express rather than on their virtuosity. Cezanne emphasized this point in a letter to his mother: 'I must go on working, but not in order to attain a finished perfection which is so much sought after by imbeciles. And this quality which is commonly so much admired is nothing but the accomplishment of a craftsman, and makes any work produced in that way inartistic and vulgar. I must not try to finish anything except for the pleasure of making it truer and wiser.'[1]

The two elements, however, are always dependent upon each other. There is a certain intrinsic quality manifest in every product of craft:

> All craftsmen share a knowledge. They have held
> Reality down fluttering to a bench;

and poets are also craftsmen:

> So language, smithied at the common fire,
> Grew to its use; as sneath and shank and haft
> Of well-grained wood, nice instruments of craft,
> Curve to the simple mould the hands require,

---

[1] Quoted by Gerstle Mack, *Paul Cézanne*, p. 199.

Born of the needs of man.
The poet like the artisan
Works lonely with his tools; picks up each one,
Blunt mallet knowing, and the quick thin blade,
And plane that travels when the hewing's done;
Rejects, and chooses; scores a fresh faint line;
Sharpens, intent upon his chiselling;
Bends lower to examine his design,
If truly made,
And brings perfection to so slight a thing
But in the shadows of his working place,
Dust moted, dim,
Among the chips and lumber of his trade,
Lifts never his bowed head, a breathing-space
To look upon the world beyond the sill,
The world framed small, in distance, for to him
The world and all its weight are in his will.[1]

In everyday life—in conversation, letter-writing, dressing, dancing and love-making—the two are inextricably mingled.

Technique is concerned with the overcoming of the inherent stubbornness of material, which resists human shaping. It is no more the whole of men's expression of feeling than efficient execution is the whole of an act, or than an assertion of fact is the whole of what men say about reality. The stubbornness of material is the material limitation, the material necessity of expression.

Although technique enters into economics and science it is primarily an exercise of the senses. The mower works by the feel of his scythe, the craftsman in wood or stone by his eye, and the feel of hammer and chisel. Even the skill of the surgeon or mechanic, though directed by knowledge, is the exercise of touch and sight.

[1] V. Sackville-West, *The Land*, pp. 81–2.

Art is the expression of the intrinsic qualities men find in reality—in things, persons, events or life as such. To use the phraseology of culinary art, the artist is concerned to bring out the flavour of the universe. The quality found in one particular reality is always expressed by associating it with the quality of another particular reality. Burns expresses the quality he-finds in his love, in a particular mood, by associating her with a June rose, and a certain verbal cadence. Her quality is symbolized by this association; the quality of the image and the cadence jointly embody it, and so convey it to us. Similarly, Beethoven expresses the intrinsic quality of life, as in a certain mood it comes to him, by associating it with the melodies and harmonies of the Fifth Symphony; the intrinsic quality of the music embodies and so conveys to us the quality of his mood.

Now quality is not atomic. The essence of art is that it expresses the wholeness of things. Thus, even a still life of fruit expresses, in its degree, the quality of the universe as felt by the artist. So, we argue, art is religious, as are value and dogma. Sometimes the religious content is explicit— the designs a Chinese bride embroidered on her trousseau, for example, directly expressed the intrinsic qualities sought in marriage.[1] Often, as in Western 'secular' painting, the religious content is less obvious, but nevertheless it is there.

If some readers find it difficult to follow us here we would suggest once more that their difficulty springs from too narrow a conception of what religion is. Religion is a putative participation of men in reality, a participation mediated by action, concept and expression. It is not confined to any particular type of social situation, nor to any particular set of values, dogmas and artistic forms. By defining art as the religious element of emotional expression

[1] Chiang Yee, *A Chinese Childhood*, pp. 135–6.

we are not trying to hang round the neck of the artist the
stole of a priest, but only to show that their work is objectively comparable.[1] The Christian priest is, in one aspect,
a kind of artist, for he is concerned to express in appropriate
symbols the intrinsic qualities of reality, which he and his
flock conceive in theistic terms, and are engaged in worshipping. The imagery and cadence of hymn and psalm,
of liturgy, lesson and sermon, the shape and colour of vest-
ments, the gesture of hand and knee—these are his symbols.
But these particular symbols are only appropriate to particular occasions. The same qualities are expressed on other
occasions in Milton's poetry, Lippo Lippi's painting, and
Eric Gill's sculpture. Similarly, the qualities the communist
finds in reality are expressed not only in Party rallies with
flag, procession and song, but also in drama and architecture.[2]

There is a distinction between these examples which must
be clarified if their comparability is to be understood.
Artists are often highly specialized. Not only do painters
specialize in the intrinsic qualities of vision, musicians in
those of hearing, dancers in those of movement, and so on,
but their art is abstract in another sense also. Its relative
autonomy is emphasized, its correlation with dogma
minimized. In the symbolism of Christian worship or a
Party rally, on the other hand, there is a more immediate
concreteness. The artistic aspect is closely dependent on the
practical and intellectual aspects; and within the artistic

[1] Cf. E. M. Forster, 'The funeral of a rich person was to them what the
funeral of Alcestis or Ophelia is to the educated. It was Art'; *Howard's End*,
Chap. XI.
[2] Cf. Sir John Maynard, *The Russian Peasant and Other Studies*, 1942,
p. 423: 'The theatre is to the Bolsheviks what the Church was to the
Orthodox. The liturgy of the Church re-enacted the holy mysteries.…
Similarly the Bolsheviks required their dramatists and producers to show
to their people the great events and characteristic life and aims of the
Revolution.'

aspect itself there is a mingling of poetry, music, rhetoric, and dance.

Christian, and some non-Christian, artists divine in reality, mystical, i.e. insensible, qualities, such as 'the light that never was on sea or land'. Their symbols therefore suggest these insensible qualities, they try to manifest a 'mystery'. But not all art suggests mystery, any more than all dogma is transcendent. Much art is confined to the divination and embodiment of sensible qualities. So-called 'secular' art is the parallel in the emotional aspect of non-transcendent dogmas.

In applying the distinction between craft and symbolism to primitive societies, we find that, as in the practical and intellectual aspects, no general distinction is given in the facts, but particular distinctions are made which are comparable.

(g) CONCLUSION

We distinguish then between culture, the social activities which are the positive content of social relations, and structure, the negative form which makes relations possible by limiting them. Structure is sectional as well as general, i.e. it maintains diversity as well as uniformity, and allows of the process of social separation. We find in all relations practical, intellectual and emotional aspects, together with material and religious aspects and structural form. Science and philosophy, economics and morality, technique and art, can, we argue, be distinguished in all societies, though their relative autonomy is much greater in civilized than in primitive societies. Philosophy, morality and art are always religious, that is they refer to a supposed ultimate reality, but they can be objectively observed. The six elements and three forms of society which we distinguish may be diagrammatically summarized thus:

	Practical aspect	*Intellectual aspect*	*Emotional aspect*
Material aspect	Economic element	Scientific element	Technical element
Structural form	Legal form	Logical form	Conventional form
Religious aspect	Moral element	Philosophical element	Artistic element

These elements and forms are, we repeat, abstractions. In every relation six elements and three forms can be traced. A relation may be predominantly economic or predominantly moral; predominantly scientific or predominantly philosophical; predominantly technical or predominantly artistic; and the form of limitation may be predominantly legal, or predominantly logical or predominantly conventional: nevertheless the other elements and forms enter into it. To speak of the economic relations, governed by law, between a grocer and his customer, is not to exclude the other elements and forms, but to contrast the dominance of economics and law in that relation with the dominance of science and logic in the relation between two scientists, or with the dominance of art and convention in the relation between lovers.

CHAPTER IV

PRIMITIVE AND CIVILIZED SOCIETY

(a) COMPLEXITY

THE greater autonomy of the elements which we have observed to exist in large-scale societies is but one manifestation of their greater specialization and variety. In all societies there is some specialization. Even in the most primitive groups there is a division of labour between men and women, between young and old; and there are corresponding differences in knowledge and skill. But in large-scale societies there is far greater specialization. A primitive Nyakyusa is farmer and builder, priest and lawyer, artist and philosopher, and perhaps doctor or smith or administrator, all in one; a civilized man rarely fulfils more than one of these functions. More distinctions are made by civilized men than by primitives, and this implies greater intellectual specialization. Not only are there specialist scientists in our society, but specialist mathematicians, physicists, biologists, and so on. Similarly, there is a multiplication of techniques and of technical specialists.

Just as there is division of labour between contemporaries, so there is division of labour between generations. One generation, by means of the capital it inherits, further develops the resources at its disposal. So also, on the basis of the knowledge and skill it inherits, it carries out scientific research and makes further inventions. In each case development is dependent upon the work of the previous generation. We, as sociologists, build on the foundations laid by Tylor and Durkheim, Malinowski and Radcliffe-

Brown. Thus, in its historical moment, specialization is material development (*vide infra*, p. 101).

Like contemporary specialization, material development increases with scale. In primitive societies there is little specialization between the generations. Always there is some: inventions are made, facts are observed, and the knowledge of them passed down. Cattle and crops may multiply, and a greater variety and quantity of seed and of breeding stock be passed on than was inherited. But the development is relatively slight. In civilized societies it is much greater. The rapid economic, scientific and technical development of our society is one of its most marked characteristics. With us this development is recent, but a large-scale society in which development has slowed down considerably is conceivable. The only necessity is that there should be a high degree of specialization between the generations, at some period in its history. So long as a society is expanding, however, there must be material development.

All material change is not development, any more than all differences in occupation, in knowledge and in skill are specialization. Specialization is *complementary* diversity. Differentiation, instead of involving division of labour between contemporaries and generations, may involve conflict. Then it is non-complementary diversity. To this we shall return in the next chapter.

The religious parallel to specialization is religious variety, by which we mean complementary religious differences. In the religious aspect, as in the material, differentiation in primitive societies is mainly on the basis of sex and age. The differences between men and women are valued, as are those between young and old. Their intrinsic and necessary difference is dogmatically maintained; and the qualities of male and female, of junior and senior, are felt to be complementary and attractive. But the limits within which variety is tolerated are narrow. In civilized society they are much wider. In England, for example, a considerable degree of variety is valued. Polemics against the evil of a 'dead uniformity' are frequent, and the proverb that it 'takes all sorts to make a world' is not only an expression of resignation to unavoidable differences. It is widely held that absolute truth cannot be fully stated in human speech; that creeds, while they may point to the nature of reality, cannot contain it; and that all of them, therefore, are in some degree relative. Hence variety of formulation is regarded as necessary for the revelation of truth. This dogma of relativity is paralleled in the emotional aspect by romance —the fascination of the unfamiliar—which permeates our society. Its force is proved by the emphasis on novelty in advertisements and by the prosperity of tourist agencies, as well as by the attraction of history and of anthropology. Variety attracts partly because it illuminates the familiar. All symbolism is an association of qualities, but to the romantic artist intrinsic quality is further revealed by the association of a wide range of realities. Masefield's association of the 'quinquireme of Nineveh' and the 'stately Spanish galleon' with the 'dirty British coaster' brings out the quality of the coaster more clearly than would an association between it and some other familiar vessel.

The difference in the taste for variety in primitive and civilized art was borne in on us when our next-door neighbour in a Nyakyusa village, a man of substance, died. Drumming is part of the Nyakyusa death ritual, and it continued in this case, without intermission, for six days and six nights. Not only is there little technical differentiation in the Nyakyusa orchestra—three drums are the only instruments—but there was a limited variation in the rhythms. To the Nyakyusa the six days and six nights were exhilarating; to us the monotony became intolerable. By the end of the week we were remembering jobs that had to be done outside the village!

As the intensity of the wider relations increases, local styles disappear. Local manufactures are replaced by mass-produced goods; local music and drama by the productions of Hollywood. It is commonly held that variety therefore diminishes with the increase in scale. Contemporary artists view with horror the 'awful uniformity' which faces future generations. We deny that for the ordinary citizen variety diminishes with increasing scale. For the member of a small-scale society there is little variety in art. He enjoys only a very limited range of manufactures and of songs and dances. It is only in a society such as that of medieval Europe or China, or of the nineteenth-century world society (and to a less degree modern world society), in which some groups are much wider in scale than others, that the large-scale few can enjoy the variety of local styles. The civilized traveller appreciates the differences of dress and of dancing, of music and of cooking, between the relatively small-scale groups he visits, but the members of the small-scale groups do not have opportunity to share his enjoyment of variety. They know only their own art. Only the more civilized surveying the less civilized see variety in isolation.

Further, we argue, though local variety diminishes with the increase in scale, variety in the same place increases. Broken Hill with its dances from many localities is an obvious example (*vide supra*, p. 9). The Londoner's entertainment can hardly be called uniform when it includes productions of the works of Shakespeare and Shaw, of Bach and Beethoven, of Fokine and de Valois, as well as the performances of Donald Duck and Deanna Durbin. Granted that the range enjoyed by many is small, the fact that some groups only enjoy Hollywood films does not prevent there being variety in our drama. It is not in a primitive village but in French menus and in the restaurants of the cosmopolitan Soho that variety of food is found. The disappearance of local styles in dress is often given as an example of increasing uniformity, but again the appearance of uniformity is an illusion. The civilized woman, with her dance frocks and dinner frocks, street clothes and sports clothes, woollens and silks, cottons and linens, and with the rapid change of fashion, has a variety of clothes that surpasses the wildest dreams of her primitive sister. We do not suggest that local differences will vanish altogether, but rather that the size of differentiated groups increases, while art tends to be articulated more by class and profession and less on local grounds, as societies expand. For example, dialect differences in Great Britain have decreased since Shakespeare's day, but class and 'shop' differences in language are very much more marked than in small-scale societies.

In its historical moment this greater differentiation of the religious aspect is religious development. In large-scale societies there is variety in the religion of different generations, as there is variety in the religion of contemporaries, and this variety is valued. It is believed to be necessary for the revelation of truth. God, modern theologians argue, could not reveal himself all at once. The Old and New Testaments are to them the record of a progressive revelation, which still continues through the Spirit of truth. 'I have yet many things to say unto you, but ye cannot bear them now. Howbeit when he, the Spirit of truth, is come, he will guide you into all truth...'[1] So also Marxist doctrine is developed by its latter prophets, Lenin and Stalin.

In primitive societies, on the other hand, the golden age is in the past. Religious change occurs and is sometimes

[1] John xvi, 12–13.

welcomed, but the emphasis is on following traditional modes of behaviour. Most often the change is regarded as an unfortunate necessity. It is traditional dogmas which are true, traditional symbols which attract, traditional actions which are valuable.[1] The Pondo, for example, lay great stress on carrying out their *amasiko*, the traditional customs whose observance is sanctioned by the ancestors. The changes in these necessitated by living in town are believed by many to be evil, and the cause of misfortune; the new dogmas are denounced as false, the new forms of expression do not attract.[2] We do not suggest that all religious change is welcomed in civilized societies or denounced in primitive societies; we do suggest that religious change is held to be necessary in civilized societies but not in primitive societies.

Specialization and religious variety—i.e. complementary diversity, as opposed to non-complementary differences— we call *complexity*.

(b) Control of the Material Environment and Non-magicality

Not only do societies increase in complexity as they increase in scale, but they also increase in their control of the material environment. Primitives, we have argued, have a rudimentary science, but their knowledge of their material environment, whether in space or in time, is infinitesimal compared with the accumulated knowledge of a civilized society. Similarly, though they may be skilled in the cultivation of certain crops and in the care of stock, in carving, or basket-making or drumming, their techniques are always limited. There is no elaboration of skill comparable to that

[1] Cf. Malinowski, *Argonauts*, pp. 305, 327.
[2] Hunter, *op. cit.* pp. 267, 477–83, 554–6.

which produces aeroplanes and violins, modern textiles and high explosives. Proverbially, primitives lack a sense of time. So, too, the quantity of goods they produce is small in relation to the time and energy expended. To civilized men their methods seem slow and laborious, their standard of living low.

The religious correlate of increasing control of the material environment is the decrease in magic. Magic, we suggest, is a general characteristic of primitive religion which diminishes with the increase in scale.

Through all the axioms of modern science there runs the dogmatic assumption that facts have a certain autonomy within the reality they characterize. That A gets malaria and B escapes is not, we all agree, because A was 'fated', or 'willed by the gods' to get it, and B to escape. Nor could A's attack have been predicted with absolute certainty by a scientist. The conditions which made A more susceptible to malaria than B may be analysed, but the chain of causation revealed by science is never more than an infinite regress. It may be shown that it is highly probable that A not B should fall ill, but there remains a margin of chance. Science can define the mathematical probabilities, it cannot predict what will happen in a particular case.

This assertion of a universal autonomy of fact within reality, which we call chance, is a necessary condition of systematic scientific research. If events were believed to be absolutely determined in detail by the nature of meta-physical reality, then men's attention would necessarily be concentrated on religious dealings with reality, to the exclusion of such research. If A's malaria were believed to be directly due to the gods, then its material causation would not concern him; all his energies would be turned to pro-pitiating them. It is equally true, though less immediately obvious, that the general acceptance of a dogma of absolute determinism by material causation must also exclude scientific research. The behaviourists can continue their experiments only because they implicitly assume that their own behaviour is not absolutely determined. If our behaviour is absolutely determined by our experience, there can be no distinction between true and false, only between my ideas and your ideas.[1]

Magic, in its intellectual aspect, is a direct denial of the dogma of chance. It denies to fact any general autonomy within reality. The empirically observable connections of fact are held to be constantly liable to interference and direct control by reality—either by spirits or witches or by mere configurations of circumstances in which magic is immanent. The presence of magic makes sustained scientific research impossible, because unimportant.

The problem then arises of how magical belief admits of empirical observation at all. If particular connections of fact are believed to be directly determined by reality, how can empirical observation have any autonomy? How can any idea of material causation be present? When we say that the primitives do not accept the dogma of chance, we do not mean that material fact has for them no autonomy within reality at all, but only that it has no general autonomy: all situations of grave importance are magically conceived, but in situations of lesser importance empiricism has fairly free play.

A further problem remains. We have said that philosophy must always have an objective reference, and this is true in primitive life also. Religious interpretations must take account of the facts, i.e. must be in some degree tentative and empirical in regard to them. But how is it possible that a religion characterized by magical dogma can ever be thus tentative?[1] Magical dogma asserts intrinsic significance and

[1] Cf. Macmurray, *op. cit.* pp. 132–5.

power in particular configurations of circumstance. It is precisely the material characteristics of the situation to which attention is directed. How then can any material detail of it ever be empirically regarded? Dogma and observation may be reconciled first by postulating either counter-magic or some mistake in the performance. Where the efficacy of the ritual depends upon correctness in detail it is easy to argue that there has been some mistake. Secondly, much magic is esoteric and particular magicians are believed to be fallible.[1] The failure of a magical ritual may be put down to the fact that the magician who performed it was 'no good' and people remain convinced that a similar ritual carried out by some other magician would be effective. Thirdly, it is commonly foreign doctors who have the greatest reputation,[2] and thus new magic not yet proved ineffective is constantly being introduced.

We suggest, also, that the contradictions between dogma and observation may be resolved in the mind of the magician himself, in dreams. Among both Nyakyusa and Pondo[3] new medicines for use in magical situations are dreamed of. The magician's ancestors, it may be, are held to 'show them to him' in his dreams. The dream is a dogmatic revelation and so has authority within the magical situation. We suggest that it is just when the old magic has apparently failed that a novelty is thus dogmatically introduced. The magical philosophy prevents any part of the magic being openly regarded as tentative and experimental, the whole concatenation stands or falls together; and so the empirical dissatisfaction with apparent failure is suppressed by the magician, only to come out again in his dreams. In these dreams, and in the choice of magicians, there is an empirical

[1] Evans-Pritchard, *op. cit.* pp. 183–201; Hunter, *op. cit.* pp. 347–8.
[2] Evans-Pritchard, *op. cit.* pp. 195, 199–201; Hunter, *op. cit.* p. 347.
[3] Hunter, *op. cit.* p. 322.

element. Generations of such dreams have, we suggest, introduced into magical operation actually effective factors, some of which may be still unknown to our science.

Corresponding to the dogma of chance, in civilized societies, we find a non-magical morality. The exact material execution of an act is not generally taken as the sole criterion of its value. Its value also depends upon the 'spirit in which it is done'. 'Though I give all my goods to feed the poor and have not charity, I am nothing', is a characteristic moral judgement of our society. It is not that the material execution is irrelevant—charity can only be active in feeding the poor, and by similar efficient movements—but that is not taken in itself to be the unfailing residence of value. The contrast with primitive societies is marked. Pagan Nyakyusa, for example, stress the value of generosity, just as do Christians, and this value is directly maintained by religious sanctions. The stingy man in a Nyakyusa village fears 'the breath of men'— the legitimately exercised witchcraft of his neighbours— if he fails to feast them on certain occasions. Their righteous anger, will, he believes, cause illness to himself or his family.[1] But so long as meat or beer is provided on the appropriate occasions the intention of the host is irrelevant. Certain details of material execution are taken as intrinsically right.

The relative separation of the value of an act from its material execution is an essential condition of the elaboration of economics. Economics is efficient execution; the mastery of an act's material implications, the husbanding of limited resources. If the particular execution of an action is taken as the unfailing residence of that action's value, then the particular execution cannot be altered without impairing the action's value. Taboos hinder economic

[1] Cf. Godfrey Wilson. 'An African morality.' *Africa*, Jan. 1936.

elaboration. In so far as it was enforced, the taboo on usury hindered the development of trade in medieval Europe.

Correlated with the dogma of chance, and the non-magical morality of large-scale societies, is the sacramental quality of their forms of expression. Particular symbols are felt to be appropriate embodiments of intrinsic quality in particular situations—e.g. the Communion service by Christians in the situation of public worship, or the display of the Red Flag and the singing of the Internationale by communists at public meetings. But these symbols are felt neither to be exclusive nor unfailing embodiments. Intrinsic quality is not regarded as inevitably contained in the particular technical manipulation: the 'inward and spiritual grace' is relatively independent of the 'outward and visible sign'; the Red Flag may be displayed by traitors of the Revolution. So, too, no magical quality attaches to the techniques of Cezanne: his followers do not imagine that any exact reproduction of its details can assure them of participation in his artistic vision.

Primitives, on the other hand, feel particular material configurations and manipulations to be the unfailing residence of certain intrinsic qualities. They take many symbolic associations of quality as being absolute. Thunder clouds, the Nyakyusa say, are like black rams. When they fight you hear thunder; when they shake their tails—for most black rams among the Nyakyusa have a white streak beneath the tail—you see lightning. A charming poetic image we say? But to the Nyakyusa it is more than that. It is not that Anon, a man of imagination, seeing a thunderstorm approaching, coins the image for the delight of his friends, only to make a new one some other day. No, the association is taken as magical. Rams and thunderstorms are permanently and indissolubly associated; and their association—since rams fight when they meet—is of a highly dangerous quality. If a herdsman sees a thunderstorm approaching, therefore, he hurries home with his cattle, and the rest of his sheep, but the ram of the flock is left alone in the pasture 'to fight with the storm'. If the ram is taken home then the fight will be at home too, and the owner's house may be struck by lightning. So the ram is left out alone. Sometimes he prevails in his fight and the storm passes on leaving him unscathed; sometimes the storm prevails and he is struck down; but it is never worth the risk of taking him home.

The absolute character of this association involves the unfailing residence of danger in the meeting of rams and thunderstorms. Similar absolute associations we found in all the magic of the Nyakyusa which we succeeded in understanding, and we suggest that such associations are general in primitive society. Not all the symbolic associations made by the Nyakyusa had this magical character, but in all situations of emotional intensity the association was magical.

Magical associations prevent the systematic elaboration of technique, just as a magical morality prevents that of economics and magical dogma prevents that of science; and, indeed, these connections are but three aspects of the same fact. Improvements in the technique of cattle breeding among the Pondo, for example, are in part held up by such associations. In cases of sickness believed to be sent by the ancestors, the bellow of an ox or a cow as it is killed ritually is held to be essential to the recovery of the patient, for the bellowing summons the ancestral spirits to the feast.[1] Now, since a scrub beast bellows as well as a good milker or a strong draft ox, and more scrub cattle than well-bred beasts can survive on scanty pasture, improvement in the quality

[1] Hunter, *op. cit.* pp. 244, 248.

of stock is hindered. This is by no means the only reason for the failure to improve the quality of stock, but it is a factor.

A high degree of control over the material environment, then, is dependent upon a relatively non-magical religion. It is equally true that a non-magical religion depends upon a relatively great control of the environment, for, as we have seen, magic is dominant when control of the environment is weak (*vide supra*, p. 71).

In its historical moment a magical religion appears as the magical value, significance, and sanctity attached to a particular period—past, present or future. Often an institution, a topic or a mode of expression is treated as valuable, significant, and sacred because it is traditional; sometimes nowadays it is so treated because it is new. Such treatment of time is magical.

(c) IMPERSONALITY

In small-scale societies relations are largely personal. A primitive Nyakyusa worked and prayed with people he had known all his life. His society was divided into categories and groups—kinsmen and others, fellow-villagers and others, countrymen (i.e. men of the same chiefdom) and foreigners; seniors, contemporaries and juniors, men and women, etc.—and his behaviour to any person was conditioned by the categories or groups to which that person belonged, that is, his relations were in a degree impersonal. Nevertheless, most relations were also personal, for the people upon whom a man depended were not only members of particular categories and groups but also known individuals. X was not only a fellow-countryman, but that decent fellow Jo.

Large-scale societies, on the other hand, are dominated by purely impersonal relations. People know their immediate colleagues and the members of their local congregation and party group, of their sports club and literary society; but the majority of those upon whom they depend for food and clothing, of their co-religionists and fellow-country-men, are strangers to them. The relations of consumer and producer, of employer and employee, are, more often than not, unmodified by personal acquaintance.

There is a similar contrast in the intellectual aspect. Primitives know personally all those with whom they com-municate, and their conversation is largely about per-sonalities and particular events. Civilized men, on the other hand, spend much time reading books and papers whose authors they scarcely know even by name, and their intellectual system is characterized by greater abstraction. All thought is in some degree abstract—concepts 'transcend particular concrete occasions of actual happening'[1]—but for the primitive the chief interest lies in particular events and personalities; for the civilized man the cases he cites are, as often as not, the basis for, or illustrations of, wider generali-zations. Universality has indeed been taken as the essential characteristic of science and philosophy, and so markedly is it lacking in primitive societies that it is denied that they have either. We contend that primitives have both rudi-mentary science and rudimentary philosophy, but that the generalizations made by them are relatively narrow (*vide supra*, p. 70).

As for the emotional aspect, primitives again know the artists and craftsmen whose work they enjoy. They are ex-cited primarily by the personal and particular qualities of events, and, we suggest, their art emphasizes these particular qualities. In civilized societies, on the other hand, artists emphasize universal rather than particular qualities. The contrast is marked in Mr Mofolo's novel *Chaka*. The author

[1] A. N. Whitehead, *Science in the Modern World*, p. 186.

clearly intended it as a dramatic account of particular historical events. This, Sir Henry Newbolt (who writes the introduction) recognizes, but to him the interest of the novel lies in its expression of universal qualities. To him the witch doctor and his assistants are not primarily historical characters but symbols of evil. Granted that Mr Mofolo has here used a modern form of expression, his tale yet smells of the epics told round kraal fires.

In the historical, as in the contemporary, moment, primitive relations are mainly personal, civilized relations largely impersonal. Primitives take the causation of events to be personal. When misfortune occurs individual witches and sorcerers are sought and punished, or sacrifices made to certain ancestors, for they are held responsible. In civilized society impersonal causes are looked for in most cases; though there are still those who attribute all their private misfortunes to the malice of particular individuals, and the present war to the machinations of Hitler. Primitive history and legend is usually about particular heroes. What emerges about the society of the period from these tales is incidental to the story of the hero's adventures. Whether or not he is an historical character is irrelevant—the point is that history is related in purely personal terms. Primitive myths are sometimes taken by those who record them to express general qualities, but this, we suggest, is a civilized, not a primitive, interpretation. In civilized societies history and drama are also concerned with the fortunes of particular dynasties and generals, but not to the exclusion of impersonal relations. Few now find a personal interpretation of history adequate. Social relations, not individuals, are the main subject of the modern historian's study;[1]

---

[1] The change in Chinese history is emphasized by C. Y. Hsieh: 'Until recent times, standard Chinese historical works and manuals suffered greatly from the traditional practice of past dynasties in upholding blind acceptance

universal, not particular, qualities the focus of modern drama.

The distinction between personal and impersonal relations cannot be a sharp one: rather there are degrees of impersonality. An element of impersonality enters into all relations in so far as people are treated as members of a category or group, in so far as men generalize and associate qualities. We maintain that relations in the historical moment in primitive societies are largely personal because the emphasis is on individual heroes and particular events, but the relation between a living man and a dead hero never known in the flesh can never be so personal as the relation between contemporaries who are intimate and meet face to face. The relations of the living and dead never known in the flesh are comparable rather to the relations between an individual and a contemporary author whom he reads, but has never met. The relation between an author and his public is, in some degree, personal, but not so personal as the relation between that author and his friends.

(d) SOCIAL MOBILITY

Social circulation, as we saw in Chapter III, exists in every society, but the range of circulation varies with scale. In primitive societies people only move within a very small group; in civilized societies they move freely within a large group. Marriage, for example, is always exogamous—i.e. there is always some movement outside one's immediate

of the authenticity of all ancient classics. This practice...inspired records of incidents rather than of trends; of deeds of great emperors and ministers rather than of the working of institutions and systems, or the play of such forces as power groups, economic interests and popular movements. Above all it worked against the sense of historical continuity. But...writings and researches of Chinese historians during the last generation have become increasingly ecological, analytical and scientific': *The Spectator*, 1 Jan. 1943. Review by C. Y. Hsieh of Tsui Chi's *A Short History of Chinese Civilization*.

family group—but the choice of a mate may be more or less limited. By the degree of social mobility we mean the size of the group within which people move freely. Mobility may be limited vertically by geographical barriers and poor means of communication; or horizontally by class or caste or race, or by barriers of sex and age. Closed age and sex groups are comparable to a caste system. In the historical moment the limitation of mobility is the principle of inheritance. A man's race is determined by his parentage; often his class also is largely so determined, and sometimes his occupation. Where a caste system exists his position is largely fixed by his birth.

In comparing the degree of mobility in different societies we can compare only the range of movements of a similar kind. It is obvious, for example, that a holiday visit to Switzerland is not comparable with the adoption of Swiss nationality, neither is a temporary liaison comparable with marriage. The movements which are comparable are those by which a similar degree of intensity (*vide supra*, p. 26) is transferred from one relation to another. We can compare the range of marriage in two societies if marriage in each involves a similar change in the intensity of relations; or the range of holiday visits on which the visitors enter into similarly intense relations with the inhabitants of the country they visit.

The rate of circulation in societies, that is, the number of movements per head of the population during a given period, varies (*vide infra*, p. 128); but that does not affect the degree of mobility,[1] which is measured by the proportion of movements of a given kind within a given circle, to the total number of movements of that kind in the whole society, e.g. the proportion of marriages outside Great

[1] Here and on the following point we differ from Sorokin; cf. P. Sorokin, *Social Mobility*.

Britain to the total number of marriages entered into by the inhabitants of Great Britain.

We deny that the amount of change in status possible in a society is a measure of the degree of mobility in it. Neither the amount of stratification of a society nor the geographical area it covers is a measure of its size: a society of given size may be more or less stratified and cover a greater or less area. Thus in measuring mobility it is not the vertical any more than the geographical *distance* which men move which is relevant, but the *size of group* within which they move freely.

In comparing the degree of mobility in different societies, therefore, we compare the size of groups within which a similar proportion of movements of a similar kind are made, e.g. the size of group within which 60 % of the total marriages of that society are made. Mobility may be increased by an increase in the size of group within which people move at all; or by an increase in the proportion of the more distant to the narrower moves (as when out of the total number of marriages of British citizens the proportion of marriages with other nationals increases); or by a change in the kind of movements made. When a greater degree of intensity is transferred than formerly, as when Englishmen begin to marry in countries which formerly they only visited as tourists, there is an increase in mobility.

(e) NECESSARY CONNECTIONS

Complexity, control of the material environment and non-magicality, impersonality and mobility are not only observable in our own and other large-scale societies; they are necessarily connected with one another and with largeness of scale.

Complementary diversity is, as we have seen (*vide supra,*

p. 46), the positive content of relations—people trade neither when their products are identical nor when the things they value are totally different, but when their products are different, yet valued by both. So also in the intellectual and emotional aspects it is difference within a wider uniformity which makes men communicate with one another. A high degree of specialization and variety is thus the basis for a large number of relations, i.e. for largeness of scale.

It is only through specialization, moreover, that control of the material environment can be achieved, for it is physically impossible that one individual should master all knowledge, or be skilled in all the techniques of our society, or that we should produce what we do without division of labour. It is likewise impossible that one generation should make the intellectual discoveries [1] and technical inventions, or accumulate the wealth, which together afford such control of the material environment as our society has. 'Long-term policies' together with scientific and technical development, i.e. differentiation in time, are essential to such control.

Control of the material environment, in its turn, makes largeness of scale possible. Without developed communications, which is a form of control over the material environment, there can be no intense relations between groups distant in space: without capital accumulation, without writing or painting, musical scores or choreography, without durable manufactured goods, there can be no intense relations between groups distant in time.

Largeness of scale makes specialization profitable, informative, and technically helpful. In a very small community a doctor or a smith, for example, cannot be a

[1] Cf. A. N. Whitehead: 'No one man, no limited society of men, and no one epoch can think of everything at once', *Science in the Modern World*, p. 184.

full-time specialist, for there is not sufficient demand for his services to enable him to pay for food, house, clothing, etc., if he produces none of these things for himself. In a larger community he can specialize with profit. Similarly, the particular knowledge or skill of a primitive specialist makes only a limited demand on his intellectual and sensory capacities. He can learn more than there is to learn in his particular line. Only when there is more knowledge and skill to be acquired in a society than one man can master, is full-time specialization informative and technically helpful, as Adam Smith showed.

Religious variety, non-magicality, and largeness of scale also determine one another. Without variety there is necessarily emphasis on the particular. It is only when different philosophies are there to be compared that the dogma of relativity can emerge; it is only when variety exists that it can be valued or felt attractive. If there be no religious development the particular formulations and symbols of a particular period are taken as absolute.

The dogma of chance and the dogma of relativity are likewise dependent upon one another. If all truth is believed to 'lie in a particular formulation, that is, if a creed is regarded as verbally inspired, other formulations cannot add anything; there can be no relativity of dogma. Conversely, for a creed to express truth with absolute fidelity would be to be absolutely determined by reality.

So, too, in the emotional aspect, romance and a sacramental symbolism are dependent upon one another. Apart from sacramentalism it would be impossible for men to be attracted by the unfamiliar. The quality of the unfamiliar can only be expressed in association with the familiar, for in its stark unfamiliarity it is aesthetically opaque. Romantic art overcomes this opaqueness by associating the unfamiliar with the familiar, that is, by finding in them both similar qualities. Forster's *A Passage to India* is a symbolic association of Indians and Englishmen which is only made possible by his divination of their common qualities. This divination in the unfamiliar of the qualities of the familiar is dependent upon a sacramental attitude, in the sense that intrinsic qualities are not tied to particular material configurations. Were they taken as so tied, then the unfamiliar would always remain aesthetically opaque; its material configuration is different, so then would its qualities be taken to be different. Conversely, if people have no experience of variety, they inevitably feel that certain qualities are indissolubly associated with certain symbols, and cannot be otherwise expressed.

In the practical aspect the same argument applies. So long as value lies in the material details of action, variety cannot be valued; if people have no experience of variety they attach a magical value to the details of action.

A magical religion limits the range of relations in their material aspect by limiting the control of the material environment. It also limits them in their religious aspect, for where emphasis is on the particular, religion cannot be widely inclusive. The magic of blood—that is, absolute determination by particular facts of kinship or race—for example, limits intense relations with other groups. The segregation policy in South Africa is based on the belief that Europeans and Africans are fundamentally different, and that therefore relations between them are wrong. It is a dogmatic and symbolic denial of their unity, and of the value of their close relations. Similarly, the Nazis postulate an absolute difference between so-called 'Aryan' and Jew or Slav, and their policy is directed towards reducing the intensity of relations between 'Aryan' on the one hand and Jew and Pole on the other. In both cases it is not only that equality between the different groups is denied, but relations between them are held to be corrupting. In South Africa it is not only intermarriage that is frowned on; extra-marital relations between white and black are a criminal offence.

Attempts to limit intense relations are sometimes confused with the value of variety. Those who urge that 'Africans should develop on their own lines' are often more concerned with segregation than with differentiation. Their object would not be attained if some Europeans adopted African customs and some Africans European customs. Moreover, as we have already shown, variety increases instead of diminishing with greater intensity in the wider relations.

We argue then that religious variety, non-magicality and largeness of scale determine one another. One cannot be fully attained without the others. How the religion of race then exists in the modern world is a paradox still to be examined.

In a large-scale society it is physically impossible that everyone should know everyone else, face to face. A high degree of impersonality is therefore unavoidable. Impersonality is also inseparably connected with non-magicality. Conversation is mainly about particular persons and particular events only when significance is believed to lie mainly in particular events. Causation is taken to be particular and personal only when the dogma of chance is denied. The impersonality of economic relations, so often deplored by moralists, is, we argue, a necessary condition of the decline in the belief in witchcraft.

Besides being a condition of, and conditioned by, a non-magical religion, impersonality is directly correlated with the control of the material environment. The development of science depends upon wide generalization and abstraction; mass production depends upon treating people not as individuals but as members of categories and groups.

Differentiation also, in so far as it involves subordination within a group, i.e. in so far as the diversity is complimentary, involves impersonality.

Increasing mobility, though it tends to reduce rather than to increase impersonality, is a condition of increasing intensity in the wider relations. The relations of exclusive groups are necessarily limited in intensity. Mobility tends to increase the number of face-to-face relations, and personal contact always adds to the intensity of a relation. Mobility between classes, and age and occupational groups, also increases intensity by forming additional links between them. In a primitive society the relations between men and women, for example, cannot be so intense as they can be in a civilized society where the sex division of labour is less marked. It is complementary diversity which makes for intense relations (*vide supra*, p. 46). When there is no mobility between the work-groups of men and women the diversities between them are partly non-complementary. When, for example, women spent their days working wool tea-cosies and antimacassars and visiting, and never studied law or medicine, engineering or sociology, the relations between them and their husbands who did study these things were necessarily limited. Woolwork tea-cosies cannot be a subject of discussion between husband and wife comparable to a common profession; the wife rather talks to another woman who appreciates the fine points of embroidery, the husband to another man of his profession. Exclusive groups have not sufficient in common with outsiders to communicate freely with them; in other words, the diversities between them are partly non-complementary.

Differentiation makes mobility worth while—if all the groups in a society were identical no one would move (*vide supra*, p. 60)—and mobility makes differentiation possible by allowing of tolerance, relativity and romance. As

Mannheim shows, it is only when people move into a group other than that in which they grew up that they realize the relativity of thought. 'That which within a given group is accepted as absolute appears to the outsider conditioned by the group situation, and recognized as partial. . . . This type of knowledge presupposes a more detached perspective.'[1] Similarly, mobility fosters tolerance and romance.

A high degree of mobility is a condition of a high degree of control of the material environment,[2] for rigidity is a limitation of the full use of human resources. Human beings are not born with equal ability, and ability is not wholly determined by heredity. When occupation is determined by a rigid caste system much potential skill, knowledge and wealth is wasted. When, for example, a colour bar excludes Africans from education the society loses many skilled technicians, scientists and business men who might otherwise have been produced. The U.S.A. would have been poorer without Paul Robeson and Washington Carver, yet were the colour bar in the States more rigid than it is, these men could not have found scope for their abilities. In so far as a society limits the use of the ability of its members it limits its use of resources. Colour and sex bars in industry inevitably limit production. It is observable that in wartime when increased production is required colour-bar restrictions are relaxed (as on the copper mines of Northern Rhodesia in 1940), and women are welcomed in posts formerly reserved to men. A career open to talents is a condition of maximum control of the material environment.

There are certain material limitations on mobility. Women cannot beget children nor men bear them, and

---

[1] K. Mannheim, *Ideology and Utopia*, pp. 252–3.
[2] Cf. S. H. Frankel, *Capital Investment in Africa*, p. 143: '. . .a basic cause of the low average income of the inhabitants of the Union is the lack of "economic mobility" of its workers. . . .'

therefore the functions of the sexes are not wholly inter-changeable. Knowledge and skill cannot be acquired in a twinkling, but only through prolonged training, so mobility in skilled occupations is limited. A man cannot become a doctor or an engineer without training, and training must usually begin young. Further, ability varies, and not every-one has the talents for the occupation of their choice. In all societies of which we have any knowledge, however, social limitations of mobility exceed the limitations of material necessity, and in so far as they do so the limitation is magical.

The idea that because a man is of a different race he is fundamentally different is a dogmatic assumption; it is not an induction from observed fact. Racial dogmas are magical because they postulate an absolute connection between blood and certain types of behaviour. For example, it is maintained that a black man can never be so efficient as a white man; that a Jew by his blood is inevitably excluded from sharing the good qualities of 'Aryans'. This connection is never proved, and its advocates are neither prepared to consider the evidence, nor to experiment. They ignore, for example, the success of African engine drivers on the West Coast; they assert without experiment that Africans are unfitted for responsibility. Similarly, the assertion that women are unfitted for the diplomatic service or the Christian ministry is a dogmatic assumption which ill accords with the proved success of some women in these fields. The defence of these social limitations of mobility is that they are materially necessary. Women, it is argued, are biologically unfitted for the diplomatic service or the Christian ministry; Africans are 'temperamentally suited to perform simple machine processes',[1] and not, ap-parently, suited to skilled work; but the material necessity

---

[1] *Third Interim Report of the Industrial and Agricultural Requirements Commission*, U.G. 40–41, par. 173.

is not proved. When we speak of the magical dogmas of race and sex we do not, of course, deprecate unbiased investigation of the factors of heredity and sex; what we insist is that the Nazi dogmas of race and of sex are based on no such investigation.

We have spoken in this chapter of the 'necessary connections' between scale, complexity, control of the material environment, non-magicality, impersonality and mobility, by which we mean that these things are correlated; but the correlation is not absolute. There is a relative autonomy between these 'correlates of scale'. The degree of autonomy possible is discussed in the next chapter.

(f) Autonomy in the Narrower Relations, Subordination in the Wider

The general structural form of increase in scale is, as we saw in Chapter II, increasing autonomy in the narrower relations and increasing subordination in the wider. Specialization and variety necessarily involve autonomy in the narrower relations. It is observable that specialists have considerable autonomy within their own fields: in so far as they lack autonomy they cannot specialize. For example, objection was made to one of us using a specialized technique of the sociological field worker—that of house to house visiting with informal conversation and observation —in the mine compounds of Northern Rhodesia. The authorities urged that only the technique commonly used by compound managers and Government officials, of summoning informants to an office, and interviewing them, with a table between inquirer and informant to maintain social distance, should be used.[1] In so far as autonomy is limited in this way, specialization is limited and its advan-

[1] Lest our information be now suspect we assure readers that it was not obtained in this way.

tages lost. Specialized information is not to be obtained except by specialized techniques. The details of family life, or of religious ritual, are not revealed in an office, across a table. Since, in a large-scale society one man cannot be master of all knowledge and skill, there is an inescapable choice between allowing experts a considerable degree of freedom and limiting our control of the material environment. So, too, religious differentiation implies autonomy. Variety of value, of dogma and of expression cannot be maintained without religious freedom. The artist 'if he *feels* free, sure of himself, unafraid, easy inside...is in a favourable position for the act of creation, and may do good work....Officials...when they censor a work...do not realize that they may have impaired the creative machinery of the mind.'[1]

Specialization and religious variety, however, are complementary differences. The material differentiation is profitable, informative, and technically useful; the religious differentiation is valuable, it is a revelation of truth, and it is attractive. In the structural aspect the complementary nature of specialization and variety appears as subordination. The autonomy of the specialist and freedom of conscience are within the framework of the practical organization, or the intellectual system, or the patterns of expression of the society. The sociologist's autonomy, for example, is limited by the necessity that his concepts should be coherent not only with those of fellow-sociologists, both contemporaries and predecessors, but also with those of biologists, psychologists and other scientists. The autonomy of the artist is limited by the artistic conventions of his period and tradition. Similarly, in the practical aspect the autonomy of the business man is limited by law.

If differentiation is not so limited it cannot be informative,

[1] E. M. Forster, *Nordic Twilight*, pp. 6–7.

technically helpful, or profitable; nor can it be a revelation of truth, attractive, or valuable. Unless the sociologist observes the limitations of logic no one understands him. If the artist throws aside all artistic conventions he conveys nothing to his public. Original people have a struggle to get their ideas and visions across. They succeed in doing so only because they work within the existing logical system and conventional patterns of their society, as well as changing them. So also in the practical aspect co-operation cannot be profitable unless law is maintained.

The groups enjoying a relative autonomy may or may not have a territorial basis. A church may be composed of people scattered through wide areas, or of all the people in one territory. The group of specialists may be an association of engineers or doctors, or it may be a territorial unit whose economy is specialized. 'Local autonomy' is the autonomy of a group whose specific bond is contiguity.

In civilized society there is a multiplication of relatively autonomous groups—trade unions, professional associations, churches, literary and artistic societies, sports clubs— they are legion. There are also innumerable relatively autonomous territorial groups ranging from the municipality to the Dominions of the British Commonwealth; from the village soviet to the constituent Republics of the U.S.S.R. But all these groups are autonomous only in their narrower relations. Their wider relations are controlled.

In primitive societies there are many small territorial groups, but these are almost wholly independent. There is some autonomy of specialists, such as that of corporations of smiths and doctors; there is a degree of local autonomy within wider political units, such as that of family, of village, and of Bemba[1] and Pondo[2] district, or Ngonde[3] fief, whose

---

[1] Richards, *op. cit.* pp. 24-5.   [2] Hunter, *op. cit.* pp. 378-82.
[3] Godfrey Wilson, *The Constitution of Ngonde*, pp. 22-5.

chief owed allegiance to a paramount chief; but the relatively autonomous groups whose wider relations are controlled are few, in comparison with those of a civilized society. Nevertheless, even slight differences in scale in primitive societies are correlated with differences in the degree of centralization. The greater centralization of Ngonde, compared with that of the Nyakyusa, is directly correlated with the fact that Ngonde society was wider in scale than Nyakyusa society.[1]

In its historical moment autonomy in the narrower relations, subordination in the wider, is structural *flexibility* combined with *traditionism*. Flexibility is the autonomy of a group from the past; traditionism is its subordination to the past. In primitive societies there is comparatively little development of law, logic and convention; what change does occur is most often, we suggest, violent, and involves considerable discontinuity. In Central Africa there was the possibility of constitutional change through the decisions of the courts, which took cognisance of particular circumstances, and so adapted the law, in some degree, to new conditions; and also through the orders of the chief in council. But the emphasis in the courts was always on following precedent, and the chief was not expected to depart far from traditional custom. So also in the intellectual and emotional aspects, there was some logical and conventional flexibility, just as there was some autonomy of specialists, and a degree of religious autonomy, but the degree of flexibility was small compared with that in a civilized society. The periods of change were, we suggest, periods of violent revolution, as when a leader like Shaka forced new laws on his people, or the migrating Ngoni conquered other groups and imposed new laws on them. With the new rulers came change in logic and convention also.

[1] *Op. cit.* pp. 8–9.

In civilized societies, on the other hand, there is continuous constitutional change through legislation. Logic and convention are also very flexible. No one feels that a generation should behave exactly as its predecessor; no one suggests that our logical formulations are final. Development is taken for granted. Violent change occurs but the rate of change possible without violence is greater than in primitive societies because succeeding generations are relatively autonomous. By the rate of change we mean the relative difference in the practical organization, the intellectual system, and the emotional patterns of succeeding generations. A change in technique, for example, which would create violent disorder in a primitive society, would not necessarily create disorder in a civilized society.

The combination of flexibility with traditionism is a necessary condition of differentiation in the historical moment. If there be no flexibility—that is, no autonomy in the narrower historical relations—there can be no change, and therefore no differentiation between generations. If there be no subordination to the past succeeding generations cannot benefit from the activities of those preceding them—the cultural heritage is lost. Flexibility and traditionism, allowing of development, are therefore a necessary condition of civilization.

Increasing impersonality is, in its structural aspect, the greater subordination of the individual to the group, of the particular to the general. Increasing mobility is the wider freedom of choice of partners and associates; that is, greater autonomy in the narrower personal relations. The individual is not bound to his position by inheritance or kinship, sex or age, in a civilized society, as he is in a primitive society.

Control of the material environment and non-magicality, being the relations of man to his environment, not of man to man, have no structural form, but, since they are conditions of large-scale society, they are indirectly correlated with autonomy in the narrower relations and subordination in the wider.

The wider scale categories and groups in a society have higher material status than the narrower, for they have greater control of the material environment. Their wealth, knowledge and skill is greater than that of their smaller scale contemporaries. They do not, however, necessarily have a higher religious status. Being less magical does not necessarily give them greater worth, wisdom and beauty in the eyes of their society. A non-racialist does not necessarily have more power than a racialist by virtue of his denial of the magic of blood; only indirectly, by the wealth he gains from co-operating with non-Europeans, does he gain greater power.

Equality cannot exist in any society because leadership is a social necessity and, though in civilized societies different people have high status in different fields, there must yet be some co-ordination of specialists, some unified control. Maximum equality of opportunity is, however, a condition of maximum control of the material environment. The ideal of equality is an illusion, but maximum mobility is a necessity in a large-scale society.

Increasing control of the material environment allows of considerable increase in individual differences in the quantity of goods consumed, in knowledge, and in skill. Such differences are much greater in modern, than in old, Central Africa. But how far differences increase depends also upon the values of the society: consumption may be limited by rationing, or limitation of incomes; education may be more or less democratic. Further, the increase cannot continue indefinitely. A society of maximum scale must make maximum use of the potentialities of its members.

If some sections are poor, ignorant, and unskilful, the scale of that society, and consequently the consumption, knowledge, and skill of its members, is limited. Therefore differences in consumption, knowledge, and skill will diminish as a society approaches maximum scale, though minor differences, due to innate capacity, will remain. Very small and very large scale societies have minimum differences in consumption, knowledge, and skill; medium scale societies may have larger differences. It does not, however, follow that differences in status necessarily increase as a society develops from very small to medium size. Social status is always relative, and it is wealth, knowledge, and skill *relative to members of the same society* which determine status. To a European, the differences in food, housing, and clothing of rich and poor Nyakyusa seem slight; but to them, the presence or absence of beef, beer, and milk, at a meal, makes the difference between a Savoy dinner, and bread and cheese at an A.B.C. to a Londoner. The possession of three cows, which makes it possible for him to marry, is the equivalent to a Nyakyusa of £500 a year to an English intellectual. The rich man's surplus goods give him control over others in primitive, as in civilized, society: his generosity in distributing land, cattle, and food gives him power and prestige. Though the quantity of goods he controls appears small by civilized standards, nevertheless, they spell power. Thus a Nyakyusa father owning two or three cows has more power over his son than an English father owning a hundred head. Similarly, differences in knowledge and skill which appear slight to a civilized man bulk large to a Nyakyusa.

Increase of scale then, though necessarily involving greater centralization, produces not less but more freedom in personal relations; not less but more local autonomy;[1]

[1] Cf. E. H. Carr, *Conditions of Peace*, p. 63: '...The very process of concentration and centralization...inevitably ends by setting up a com-

not greater inequality but greater mobility. The freedom of a primitive man is limited at every point by the pressure of neighbours and kinsmen, living and dead, from whom he cannot escape. He has little privacy. His position in society is largely fixed by sex, age, and blood. The freedom of the civilized man from neighbours and kinsmen, and from the immediate past, is much greater than that of a primitive; not only does he live relatively aloof in his house, but he can escape the living by moving, and he does not cut himself off from his ancestors by changing his habits. On the other hand, he is dependent upon distant groups—upon banks and cartels, upon his heritage from ancient Greece and Rome, Palestine and China—in a way in which a primitive man is not dependent.

As we have shown, subordination in the wider relations, autonomy in the narrower, operates in the intellectual and emotional aspects as in the practical. Here we differ from those who suggest 'cultural' (i.e. intellectual and emotional) independence for the nations of Europe, combined with economic and political centralization. Intellectual and emotional centralization already in fact exist. The premises of Einstein are accepted in London and Moscow, as well as in Berlin and New York. The artistic conventions of China are influencing English ballet. But this does not exclude a high degree of specialization and variety, some of which has, and will continue to have, a local habitation.

Structure is nothing but the form of culture and there can be no separation of the two. Increase in scale automatically involves autonomy in the narrower relations, subordination in the wider—there is no choice; but as we have already argued (*vide supra*, p. 108) societies may be wider in scale in some respects than in others, and therefore there may be

pensating process of devolution for the more far reaching and more ubiquitous the activities of Government, the more necessary does it become to decentralize control in the interests of efficient administration.'

more autonomy in the narrower relations in some respects than in others; subordination in the wider relations in some respects and not in others. The maintenance of local autonomy is simply the maintenance of local specialization and variety; a government which allows of no local differentiation is a small-scale, not a large-scale, phenomenon.

(g) The Evidence from Central Africa

The characteristics of civilized society cited here are becoming more and more evident in Central Africa. Not only is there an observable difference between different groups in Central Africa at the present time but, in written records and in the memory of the living, there is proof of the change. The evidence has already been referred to in Chapter 1, and in illustration of the preceding argument, but it is convenient to summarize it here.

The range of material relations has expanded enormously, and includes close co-operation between European and African in mines, in agriculture, in administration, in commerce, and in domestic work. Religion is more widely inclusive—in some areas 45 % of the population profess a world religion (*vide supra*, p. 12)—but racialism is strong and limits religious inclusiveness. Though the main barrier is between black and white, a pseudo-racialism operates within the white group also. The British version of the Nazi doctrine of the 'Herrenvolk'—British Israelitism—flourishes, and asserts the sacred destiny of the 'Anglo-Saxon people' to dominate all 'lesser breeds'.

The Europeans in Central Africa are highly specialized, and there is far more specialization among the Africans themselves than formerly (*vide supra*, pp. 4–5); but the mass of Africans are still unskilled labourers, engaging in agricultural and industrial work alternately, as they circulate from country to town and back.

There is great diversity of religion. Racialist and non-racialist, pagan and Christian, Mohammedan and materialist, live side by side, and the Christians are divided into innumerable sects. Much of this diversity is non-complementary—racialists and non-racialists pursue values and maintain dogmas which flatly contradict one another. Between pagans and Christians and Mohammedans, there is a degree of mutual toleration. We found, for example, in BuNyakyusa, that the few Mohammedans in the district got on well enough with their neighbours; that one member of a family might be Christian and his views be respected by pagan relations. If a man or woman who held some pagan office were baptised their place was usually taken by a brother or sister or cousin without much difficulty. At a pagan twin ritual we attended it was explained that the doctor in charge was handing over to her sister, since she, the former doctor, was a catechumen, and about to be baptised. She had taught her sister the necessary medicines and procedure. Only in the case of eldest or only sons, who traditionally should inherit the wives of their father, was there great opposition to conversion by pagan relatives. Many Christian missionaries are equally tolerant, holding with the late Archbishop of Canterbury that 'the conscience of the heathen man is the voice of God within him—though muffled by his ignorance';[1] but, as we have seen (p. 16), there are still some to whom a responsible non-Christian is 'that pagan'.

Within the Christian group itself relations between Pro-

---

[1] William Temple, *Readings in St John's Gospel*, First Series, p. 10. The passage continues: 'All that is noble in the non-christian systems of thought, or conduct or worship is the work of Christ upon them and within them. By the word of God—that is to say by Jesus Christ—Isaiah, and Plato, and Zoroaster, and Buddha, and Confucius conceived and uttered such truths as they declared. There is only one divine light; and every man in his measure is enlightened by it.'

testant and Roman Catholic, and between the missionary churches and independent African Churches, are often strained. We know one Protestant missionary who openly taught that Catholic priests were emissaries of Satan, and there is frequently competition between different Christian sects for converts and control of schools.

The present religious diversity of Central Africa therefore is partly complementary—that is, there is increasing variety, which is an aspect of the increase in scale—and partly non-complementary difference. To these non-complementary differences we shall return in the next chapter.

In the historical moment, as in the contemporary, there is increasing differentiation. European policy nowadays is aimed at developing existing institutions rather than making a break with the past. The policy of 'indirect rule' introduced in Tanganyika in 1926, and later extended to Nyasaland and Northern Rhodesia, is a method of administration through traditional authorities. Where formerly the Government had aimed at reducing the power of African chiefs its policy was reversed. For example, until 1933, no paramount chief, such as had traditionally existed, was recognized by the British administration in Ngonde. Changes made in 1924 were in 'no way intended to revivify or perpetuate governance by Native chiefs'. But in 1933, the traditional political institutions of Ngonde were taken as the basis of administration. The Kyungu was now recognized as 'Paramount Chief', with an appeal court, and five 'subchiefs' under him.[1]

Agricultural experts are becoming more chary of introducing sudden changes in African agricultural techniques, for, they say, Europeans lack knowledge of local conditions, and indiscriminate application of European techniques, such as the use of the plough, has, in some places, had

[1] Godfrey Wilson, *The Constitution of Ngonde*, p. 69.

disastrous results. Rather they seek to control and develop the existing agricultural systems, controlling cutting in the *chitemene* areas, enforcing the traditional system of contour ridging among the Nyakyusa, and gradually experimenting with new techniques and new crops.[1]

In the religious aspect also the modern emphasis is on development rather than on abrupt change. Christian missionaries are seeking to base their teaching on traditional African beliefs. They emphasize the development of religion in Israel and plead for a corresponding development in Africa;[2] tribal traditions are to some the 'African's Old Testament'. Experiments have been made with Christian initiation schools for adolescents in Masasi, in which traditional and Christian teaching are fused;[3] and with the initiation of Christians as tribal elders among the Meru.[4] The degree in which missions seek to build on the past, rather than to break with it, varies greatly—the giving of bride wealth by Christians is still forbidden by some Churches, for example, and participation in traditional initiation schools is generally frowned upon—but the necessity of 'preserving what is good' in African tradition is widely accepted. Detailed study of the rituals of Christian families at birth, marriage and death show that in practice old and new are inextricably intertwined.[5]

Control of the material environment in Central Africa has increased enormously. Railway, motor and air trans-

---

[1] G. C. Trapnell and J. N. Clothier, *op. cit.* pp. 58–62. Also conversations with the late W. Eustace, Assistant Agricultural Officer, Rungwe District, Tanganyika.

[2] Cf. E. W. Smith, *African Beliefs and Christian Faith*.

[3] Cf. W. V. Lucas, Bishop of Masasi, 'The educational value of initiatory rites,' *The International Review of Missions*, April 1927.

[4] Cf. E. M. Holding, 'Women's institutions and the African church', *The International Review of Missions*, July 1942.

[5] Unpublished material on the Nyakyusa. Cf. Hunter, *op. cit.* pp. 158–9, 213–20, 483–5, 527–34.

port have largely replaced the porter; copper and gold mines equipped with the latest machinery replace primitive workings. The immense achievements of medical science make it possible for Europeans to maintain their health in a tropical climate. But the application of civilized wealth, knowledge and skill is patchy, and the bulk of the Africans are still, by civilized standards, very poor, very ignorant, and very unskilful. As we have seen, malnutrition is general and increasing; erosion threatens to destroy the fertility of large areas; and everywhere there is much preventable ill-health.

Increase in control of the material environment has been dependent upon a relatively non-magical religion, but non-magicality, like the development of wealth, knowledge and skill is patchy. The proportion of occasions on which Africans attribute misfortune to witchcraft and sorcery is diminishing;[1] and traditional magical rituals are often omitted. Nyakyusa Christians, for example, no longer perform the traditional magic at the birth of twins, and at the initiation of a girl. 'Some pagans, seeing that we do not fall ill, leave these rituals too.' Nevertheless, belief in magic is still general. Not only do old beliefs survive, but Christianity is interpreted by many in magical terms.[2] Europeans are mostly non-magical about disease and in their specialist professions, but they hold to the magic of blood. Material development is generally accepted as good, but in certain situations men find value, significance and beauty in traditional forms alone. To many Europeans, for example, the

[1] Accusations of witchcraft and sorcery are an expression of opposition, and in so far as the oppositions of everyday life are exacerbated by dis-equilibrium (*vide infra*, Chap. v), the number of accusations may have increased—we do not know. Nevertheless, we suggest that the *relative* importance of magic is declining and that of science increasing. Here we differ from Dr Audrey Richards, cf. 'A modern movement of witch-finders', *Africa*, Oct. 1935.

[2] Monica Hunter, 'An African Christian morality', *Africa*, July 1937.

traditional pattern of race relations is ultimate and unchangeable.

Since, in Central Africa, so many more people are in relation than formerly, it is impossible for them all to know each other, and many relations are wholly impersonal. One old chief complained to us that it was very difficult for him to do justice nowadays, because he and his councillors no longer knew all the individuals who came to court, personally, as they used to do. When they knew everyone concerned, their families and circumstance, it was much easier to distinguish truth from falsehood, than when the case involved strangers. The impersonality of relations is most marked across the racial barrier. To many Europeans an African is not an individual, but simply a member of another race. Often even in private households a servant's name is not used, he is just 'boy'; and in newspaper reports of accidents, etc., when European names are given, a non-European is often just 'a native'.

Africans, now having wider experience, make wider generalizations, and in every village school the rudiments of mathematics, the most abstract form of thought, are taught. Where advanced technical and scientific teaching is given the medium is usually English, partly because the vocabulary of the vernaculars is inadequate to convey such abstract ideas. In dogmatic teaching vernaculars are largely used, but the content of traditional words changes. The meaning a Nyakyusa pastor gives to the Nyakyusa word for God (Kyala), for example, is different and more abstract than the content given it by his fathers, to whom it meant a particular ancestor. Clan histories and praise songs, glorifying the adventures of particular individuals, are no longer the sole historical training of young Africans.

The group within which Africans move freely is much larger than it used to be. Marriage outside the chiefdom, formerly rare among the Nyakyusa, is now common, as are intertribal marriages in town.[1] Men travel as far as the Rand to work, and position is less determined by inheritance than formerly. A younger son, for example, may earn cattle and marry as soon as his elder brother, which used to be an unheard of proceeding. A man's religion is not determined by birth as it is when his only gods are his ancestors, his only priests the seniors of his family. Nevertheless, mobility is strictly limited vertically by the barrier of race. Inter-marriage is not legally possible between Europeans and Africans in Nyasaland and Northern Rhodesia, though extra-marital relations between the races is not a criminal offence as it is in the Union. Many skilled occupations are not open to Africans, and opportunity for more advanced education, technical and general, is lacking. Social inter-course between the races is frowned upon.

We have noted elsewhere the increasing centralization of Central African society—the loss of power by headmen and minor chiefs at the expense of paramount chiefs, and the central administration; the control of the various Terri-tories by Great Britain; the subordination of local industry and agriculture to world copper, coffee, and tea agreements (*vide* pp. 7, 140). There is at the same time greater freedom from kinsmen and neighbours.[2] A young man who is energetic can earn cattle for himself fairly rapidly, he is no longer dependent upon inheritance, or on slow accumula-tion by serving a chief. A Christian or Mohammedan does not believe himself to be dependent upon the good will of his family, living and dead, for supernatural blessing, as does a pagan; one who has quarrelled with his relatives, or

---

[1] Godfrey Wilson, *Economics of Detribalization*, Part II, p. 41: 'In Broken Hill today 30% of the marriages are intertribal.'

[2] Godfrey Wilson, *op. cit.* Part I, pp. 39–40; Audrey Richards, *Bemba Marriage and Present Economic Conditions*, Rhodes-Livingstone Papers No. 4 (1940), pp. 113–14.

is accused of witchcraft, can now escape by going to work at a distance.[1] Christian ministers, agricultural experts, and teachers have an autonomy within their own spheres such as did not exist in primitive society when the chief was head of the church, and director of agriculture, and sometimes organizer of initiation schools, as well as chief justice and administrator. Further, the system of indirect rule allows of considerable local autonomy. Nyakyusa retain their own law, logic and convention distinct from that of their Safwa, and Kinga neighbours. Controlling the 'Tribal Treasury',[2] into which a proportion of the taxes, court fees, fines, and other dues collected from them are paid, they have some freedom of expenditure on administration, education, health, communications, and agriculture.[3]

Machinery for constitutional change has been developed. Native courts are consciously adapting traditional law to new conditions, and one of the functions of the European District Officer is to encourage such development. Africans are beginning to expect logical and conventional change also. Traditional logical limitations and conventions are found inadequate, and though to some the golden age is still in the past, many others seek 'progress'. In the development of Nyakyusa agriculture, in the growth of the Christian Church in Ngonde, and in the recent political development of both Ngonde and BuNyakyusa, we have observed rapid change with little discontinuity. Such smooth change is, however, by no means general.

In its structural form, as in cultural content, change is partial and inconsistent. Subordination in the wider rela-

[1] Cf. M. Fortes, 'Culture contact as a dynamic process', *Africa*, Jan. 1936, p. 46; Hunter, *Reaction to Conquest*, p. 436.
[2] Cf. Tanganyika Territory, *Native Administration Memoranda No. III, Tribal Treasuries*, 1930.
[3] Expenditure of the Tanganyika Tribal Treasures in 1939 was £202,163. Tanganyika Territory, *Annual Reports of the Provincial Commissioners*, 1940.

tions is not adequate to control racial opposition, international war, or slumps on the world market; and the African is keenly aware of a lack of freedom. To discover some consistency in this apparent inconsistency is our next task.

We speak of contemporary Western society as large scale, for it is not only much larger in scale than primitive societies, but it is larger also than any of its predecessors; but in calling it large we do not suggest that it has reached its maximum size. As we saw in Chapter I the range of relations cannot extend further in this world, but the intensity of the wider relations may greatly increase. Professor Hancock puts the argument in the economic field very clearly: '...The nineteenth century...witnessed a geographical expansion of material civilization on a scale that was unprecedented in human history. The economic frontier of the western world advanced to the farthest limits of the new continents. Today there is no longer any room for advance. The frontiers are fixed....But...the conception of the welfare of nations...offers a new stimulus to take the place of the moving frontiers; it promises to an expansionist society the means of living in harmony with its own nature, even in an age when geographical expansion has reached its limits. A struggle to raise the standard of the depressed classes and the depressed areas of the world could have a dynamic effect comparable to the discovery of a new America.'[1] As we have shown, Central African society is wider in scale in some ways than in others, and an evening up of scale to the range of the wider relations would in itself be an expansion.

[1] W. K. Hancock, *Survey of British Commonwealth Affairs*, Vol. II, Part II, p. 327.

CHAPTER V

EQUILIBRIUM AND DISEQUILIBRIUM

(a) ORDINARY OPPOSITION AND DISEQUILIBRIUM

OPPOSITION exists in every society. It is of two kinds. There are ordinary oppositions and there is radical opposition. Ordinary oppositions are essentially particular and plural. They occur independently in different relations and divide people over the occupation of the existing social positions—over who is to partner whom, and over who, in particular, are to be the leaders and who the subordinates—and over the application of accepted laws, logical limitations and conventions to particular circumstances. Radical opposition, on the other hand, is essentially general and singular. No one manifestation of it can be resolved alone, for all its manifestations determine one another. It is an opposition in the social structure itself over what that structure is to become. It is a structural inconsistency affecting every social position, every law, every logical limitation and every convention. It is a disturbance of the equilibrium of society, and, as such, we call it also *disequilibrium*.

Ordinary oppositions, as we have seen in Chapter III, are controlled by social pressure and social separation. They can, therefore, recur continually without involving any social change. The existing structure of law, logic and convention continues, unimpaired, to check each opposition as it occurs and to hold it within bounds. Radical opposition, or disequilibrium, cannot be so controlled. The existing social structure is inconsistent with itself, i.e. social pressure operates in contrary directions, and continues to do so however much particular partners may be changed. It is an opposition of law and law, logic and logic, convention and convention, which only social change can resolve.

The Nyakyusa, to take a simple facet of the disequilibrium in which they are involved, lay great emphasis on hospitality. Entertaining his friends is an obligation of a rich man enforced on him not only by conventional pressure—the stingy man loses prestige—but also by fear of witchcraft, 'the breath of men', legitimately used by his cheated neighbours.[1] Hospitality is dependent upon polygyny, for only by the labour of more than one wife can a household grow and prepare enough food to entertain well. Christians are thus in a dilemma. They value both monogamy and hospitality. If a Christian take a second wife he is suspended from membership of the Church, probably lives in fear of hell fire, and is ashamed before Christians and pagans alike, for the conflict is not only between Christian and pagan, but within the Christian group itself. If he is inhospitable he is both afraid of witchcraft and again ashamed.[2] Often we saw Christian wives struggling to get through more work than they could manage, in order to entertain as they wished to do. The opposition can only be resolved by social change, economic or religious. Either there must be greater division of labour so that the well-to-do may buy some of their food, more provision of water in the villages, mechanized milling to replace the laborious hand grinding, and the employment of servants; or, on the other hand, the abandonment either of hospitality, or of monogamy. Radical opposition is even less tolerable than ordinary opposition, and social change always does and always must follow its occurrence. In BuNyakyusa, adjustment in the situation described was in

---

[1] Cf. Godfrey Wilson, 'An African morality', *Africa*, Jan. 1936, p. 85.
[2] Cf. Monica Hunter, 'An African Christian morality', *Africa*, July 1937, pp. 275-6.

fact beginning. A few well-to-do Christians employed youths to help in field work, and in fetching wood and water; while coffee, requiring relatively little preparation, was offered to visitors rather than home-brewed beer.

Radical opposition is always muddled; that is to say, conflicting laws, contradictory concepts and disharmonious conventions are supported by the same people. Men are divided against themselves as well as against their neighbours. It is only by being muddled, or in more philosophical language, generally unrealized, that radical opposition can exist at all. For it to be generally, i.e. consistently, realized in action, concept, and expression is for it to be overcome. It is a struggle between nascent and opposing social structures over which is to prevail. In action its general realization is the organized establishment of one, and consequently the organized exclusion of the other nascent legal structure. In concept its general realization is the consistent acceptance of one, and consequently, the consistent rejection of the other nascent logical structure. In expression its general realization is a sustained adherence to one, and consequently a sustained disengagement from the other nascent conventional structure. The general, i.e. the consistent, realization of disequilibrium, for the radical opposition that it is, is the social change that resolves it. Conceptually it is impossible for the members of any society generally to realize that a radical opposition exists, but only that it has existed. Both of the nascent structures cannot be consistently supported in the same society, for flatly contradictory policies cancel out. In South Africa, for example, there cannot be *both* total segregation of the races and the employment of Africans by Europeans. African and European cannot both remain totally isolated and work together.

So long as disequilibrium lasts its nature is, and must be,

generally unrealized; and the behaviour of those who tend, purblindly and on balance, to support one rather than the other of the nascent structures, is always inconsistent within itself. Both structures cannot be consistently supported by different parties, but both can, temporarily, be inconsistently supported and inconsistently opposed, at different points, by everybody.

To the members of groups opposed over a particular issue their respective policies may appear to be consistent, but, in so far as the opponents are in close relations, their opposition is in fact muddled. For the members of any group within a society in disequilibrium there are inevitably conflicts between 'party' and other affiliations. The racialist compromises in so far as he co-operates with Africans but he rarely understands this. Racialists in South Africa avowedly sought to isolate themselves from non-racialists and so gain freedom to follow a consistent racial policy, by trekking north, but their continued co-operation with Africans as servants inevitably involved contradiction of their dogma of racial purity. The degree of internal consistency possible to groups in radical opposition is the same as the degree of tenuity in the relation between them: complete consistency would involve complete separation.

Though generally unrealized for what it is, radical opposition none the less forces its existence painfully on the attention of the people involved in it. It does so by complicating the apparently ordinary oppositions of social life intolerably. It opposes people in contradictory ways. It so weakens the structure of law, logic and convention as to render the oppositions abnormally difficult to control. Breaches of law, logic and convention multiply, and social separation—i.e. movement to avoid pressure—becomes more frequent. For example, in Central Africa, circulation between village and village in the country,[1] and from job to job in town, is at present extremely rapid, and the divorce rate very high.[2]

This abnormal difficulty in maintaining order, coherence, and harmony forces on people the necessity of somehow changing the situation. As, however, it is neither understood that a radical opposition exists, nor decided in which direction it is to be resolved, this necessity is still not generally and consistently, but only particularly and inconsistently realized. The necessity of change is realized only in a number of muddled oppositions over particular issues. An apparently ordinary opposition so complicated by an underlying radical opposition as to force on people, albeit in a muddled way, the necessity of change, we call a *complex opposition*. To the people concerned it seems to be just an ordinary opposition of unusual difficulty, in no way necessarily connected with the other oppositions of the society. To the sociologist its complexity is one manifestation of a single underlying radical opposition and is thus necessarily connected with all the complex oppositions of the society.

The distinction between an ordinary and a complex opposition is not a matter of degree —of the amount of disorder, incoherence, and disharmony involved—but of kind. Ordinary opposition may be common in a particular relation without escaping intolerably from social control, and without, therefore, forcing the necessity of change on the people concerned. Complex oppositions, on the other hand, may, as we shall see more clearly in the next section, exist and prove intolerable without, at first, involving a very high degree of disorder. The points of friction, i.e. the

---

[1] Godfrey Wilson, *The Land Rights of Individuals among the Nyakyusa*, pp. 31–3.
[2] Godfrey Wilson, *Economics of Detribalization*, Part I, pp. 56–7; Part II, pp. 64–73.

points at which ordinary oppositions are most common, vary in different societies. Malinowski has shown how, in the Trobriand Islands, friction was particularly common between a boy and his mother's brother.[1] Among the Bemba of Northern Rhodesia it was common between a youth and his wife's kinsmen;[2] among the Pondo of South Africa between a wife and her husband's people;[3] among the Nyakyusa of South Tanganyika between co-wives. In each case the traditional social structure was such that these relatives were particularly liable to come into conflict. But though oppositions between these relatives were common they were not complex; no radical opposition underlay them; the existing laws, logical limitations and conventions were accepted and enforced. It is only within recent years that radical opposition has complicated them and led the existing social structures to be challenged. While a relatively high degree of disorder in one or two particular relations, however, is not a necessary symptom of the presence of radical opposition, and while a low degree of disorder generally is not a necessary symptom of its absence, yet a high degree of disorder generally is a necessary symptom of its presence. This can only exist if oppositions have partially escaped from social control, that is, are complex.

Just as ordinary oppositions have a material and religious content, so have the complex oppositions that manifest disequilibrium; and with both it often happens that, in some particular situation, either the one or the other content is predominant. In such cases we speak of (predominantly) moral and economic conflicts, (predominantly) dogmatic and scientific contradictions, and (predominantly) aesthetic and technical disharmonies. Ordinary conflicts, contra-

[1] B. Malinowski, *The Sexual Life of Savages*, pp. 9-13.
[2] A. I. Richards, *Bemba Marriage and Present Economic Conditions*, pp. 33-40.
[3] Hunter, *op. cit.* pp. 43, 307, 318.

dictions and disharmonies, as we have seen, are controlled by social separation and social pressure. They are dealt with, that is to say, either by a change of partners in the particular relations in which they occur, or by transforming them into oppositions between particular persons and groups, on the one hand, and some more inclusive group backed by the whole of the rest of the society, on the other, and so forcibly concluding them. Social pressure is the transformation of an opposition between particular people into an opposition between eccentricity (non-conformity), on the one hand, and law, logic, and convention on the other. The eccentricity is thereby excluded as illegal, illogical, and unconventional. If, in an ordinary opposition, the content is predominantly religious, then the eccentricity is excluded as immoral, heretical, and ugly; if the content is predominantly material then the eccentricity is excluded as inefficient, inaccurate, and unskilful.

Complex conflicts, contradictions, and disharmonies cannot be thus dealt with. Change of particular partners leaves them untouched, nor can they be forcibly concluded by the operation of social pressure. Both parties are supported in their opposition by accepted laws, logical limitations, and conventions, i.e. the operation of social pressure itself forces the oppositions on them. Either party is compelled to behave in a manner that is, from the other's point of view, to some extent illegal, illogical, and unconventional. If the content of a complex opposition is predominantly religious, then the behaviour of one party is inevitably somewhat immoral, heretical, and ugly, from the other's point of view; if the content is predominantly material then the behaviour of both parties is inevitably somewhat inefficient, inaccurate, and unskilful. These unavoidable non-conformities we call *maladjustment*.

As we have already insisted, form and content can have

no separate existence, but social facts may be regarded both structurally and culturally. Thus disequilibrium may be considered both as structural opposition or as cultural maladjustment; we may look at it primarily as conflict, contradiction, and disharmony; or primarily as unavoidable inefficiency and immorality, inaccuracy and heresy, unskilfulness and ugliness.

The underlying radical opposition of disequilibrium is always, we suggest, an opposition over scale: disequilibrium is an unevenness of scale. Opposition is muddled because the same people seek to be wider in scale in some ways than in others. If one of the nascent social structures be generally realized, then scale is no longer uneven.

(b) The Origin and Course of Disequilibrium

In its historical moment disequilibrium is uneven change; it is the failure to adjust novelty with tradition—a change in one respect without change in other respects. This unevenness is always, in one aspect, an unevenness of scale, for all social change involves some change in scale.

The impulse to change may come either from without or from within the society. Change in the external environment such as earthquake, flood, or desiccation is a cause of social change. There are also specifically social forces of change generated within society. These latter are of two kinds, positive or cultural, and negative or structural.

The positive or cultural forces of social change are new ideals, ideas and intuitions of beauty, and the discovery of new uses for material resources, of new facts and of new techniques. They draw men freely into new activities. Men change their accustomed ways of action, thought and expression not because they are compelled to do so, but because it seems to them better, more true, more beautiful, more economical, more accurate, or more skilful to do so.

The negative or structural forces are intolerable oppositions between groups and categories of people that threaten, unless some change is quickly made, to destroy law, logic and convention. These are the forces of disequilibrium. They compel men to change their behaviour by pressing on them unbearably. The more acute the disequilibrium the greater the pressure to change. Equilibrium is a fundamental social necessity; disequilibrium cannot be maintained but inevitably involves change. We have argued that disequilibrium, in its contemporary moment, is both opposition and unevenness of scale; so in its historical moment it is both compulsion to change and uneven change.

The changes that arise either in the external environment or from the positive, cultural forces of society we call *primary* changes, those that arise from the pressure of disequilibrium we call *secondary* changes.

Unevenness of scale, i.e. disequilibrium, may arise either from social change resulting from pressure of the environment, or from change for positive cultural reasons. Frequently an environmental change compels a social change in one institution, but all the other institutions of the society do not immediately change to match, and disequilibrium results. Or a new invention may be made and other institutions not be modified to match the change in technique. Thus disequilibrium may appear in a society previously in relative equilibrium.

Uneven change is to be distinguished from rapid change, i.e. relatively great change in a short time, in economic organization, scientific concepts, techniques, moral values, dogmas, and qualities expressed. Change, though it be rapid, may yet be accepted as development and involve no radical opposition. Uneven change always involves radical opposition. The larger the scale of the society the more rapid the change possible without disequilibrium. As we argued in Chapter IV, development is the historical moment of complementary diversity, and the greater the scale the greater the diversity possible without opposition.

The degree of disequilibrium varies in different societies. We have no evidence of a society in perfect equilibrium, but it is observable that the degree of disequilibrium may be increasing or diminishing; the scale of the society may be becoming more or less even. The degree of disequilibrium is the degree of unevenness between and within the correlates of scale.

Disequilibrium is inherently unstable: it involves pressure to change, and so long as it continues there must be social change. Disequilibrium is both a state of society and a force of change. As a force of change disequilibrium must always press towards its own resolution, towards equilibrium; that is implied in the fundamental necessity of equilibrium. Disequilibrium is an intolerable state of society that carries in itself the necessity of its own resolution. How, then, can disequilibrium ever increase? If each of the primary changes that cause disequilibrium, whether externally or culturally introduced into society, were made piecemeal, with an interval between it and the next, then disequilibrium could never increase. Each primary change would cause a certain disequilibrium that would then resolve itself through a number of secondary changes, before any further primary change was introduced. It often happens, however, that further external or cultural changes are introduced before the disequilibrium caused by a previous primary change has been resolved; and in this case disequilibrium increases. Moreover, it may sometimes happen that these further primary changes just about keep pace with the continual resolution of the disequilibrium; and then the disequilibrium, constantly changing its form, will remain constant in intensity. This last is a theoretical possibility of which we can quote no actual instance.

The primary changes introduced into society by changes in the external environment may involve either an increase or a decrease of scale. Those introduced for positive cultural reasons normally, if not always,[1] involve an increase of scale.

Where primary changes involve an increase of scale the resulting disequilibrium is a struggle between these wider-scale novelties and a narrower-scale traditional structure. The resolution of the disequilibrium then takes place either by the increase in the range of the narrower-scale elements to match the wider; or by a decrease in the range of the wider-scale elements to match the narrower; or by both at once.

Where relations are tenuous, reduction of scale may involve breaking them off altogether. Repeated attempts to avoid opposition by prohibiting intercourse between Europeans and Africans were made on the eastern frontier of the Cape in the eighteenth and nineteenth centuries, but they were unsuccessful, for relations between Europeans and Africans had a positive content for both groups. Government prohibitions of intercourse were ineffective.[2] Attempts to resolve disequilibrium by reduction of scale— whether it involve breaking off relations altogether, or simply reducing their intensity in one aspect—we call *social fragmentation*. It is comparable to the separation of individuals and groups in society to avoid opposition, but it is distinguished from social separation (*vide supra*, pp. 58–61) by the fact that it involves a reduction of scale. Social

---

[1] We think always, but are not prepared to be dogmatic on this point.
[2] Cf. W. M. Macmillian, *Bantu, Boer and Briton*, pp. 26, 29, 59–61, 229.

separation involves only social circulation: social fragmentation involves social change.

Disequilibrium is integral. As we have shown, its mark is the complexity of the oppositions involved, the fact that no one opposition can be resolved alone. So, also, disequilibrium cannot be resolved in one area of a society alone, only in a whole society. The resolution of disequilibrium in Central Africa, for example, depends upon its resolution in Europe. The degree of disequilibrium and the curve of its increase and decrease is not necessarily uniform throughout a society, but both degree and course in different areas are necessarily related and determine one another (*vide infra*, p. 157).

Disequilibrium involves pressure to change, and it cannot increase indefinitely; these are social necessities, but the date of resolution and the form of equilibrium achieved are relatively free. Equilibrium involves coherence between the correlates of scale, but our society may become stable, sooner or later, on a wider or narrower scale.

(c) DISEQUILIBRIUM IN CENTRAL AFRICA

Disequilibrium in Central Africa manifests itself, in the economic element, as conflict between the races over land and erosion, over markets, over wages, over the training and employment of Africans in skilled work; and in the obvious inefficiencies of 'over-production' and unemployment, together with hunger and preventable ill-health among the Africans.

Though the density of population is very low over the area as a whole, there is competition between Europeans and Africans for the most fertile and most accessible land,[1] and some 'reserves' are already inadequate for the popula-

[1] Cf. Margaret Read, 'Tradition and prestige among the Ngoni', *Africa*, Oct. 1936.

tion they carry, at the present level of agricultural development. Along the railway, and in the Tanganyika Province of Northern Rhodesia, African villages have been moved to make room for European farms,[1] and feeling is exacerbated by the fact that crowded reserves in some cases adjoin undeveloped European areas. This is most obvious in the Fort Jamieson district.[2] The land around Broken Hill, also, from which the Lenje were removed to make room for European farms, remains largely undeveloped. The Lenje have lost a profitable trade in milk, which they formerly enjoyed, and few European farmers have come to take their place.

Competition for land is closely associated with competition for markets for agricultural produce. Not only do European farmers seek a monopoly of land near railways; they seek also a monopoly of the more profitable crops. Settler pressure against the development of market crops by Africans is strong in Northern Rhodesia and, though their influence is less in Tanganyika, settlers there spoke bitterly to us of the right of Africans to produce coffee, which they felt should be a monopoly of Europeans. In neighbouring Territories monopolies for European farmers in certain crops have been secured—Africans in Kenya were forbidden to grow the more valuable coffee *arabica*; in the Union of South Africa the Maize Control Act operated against African growers, and there was agitation for further protection.[3] In Southern Rhodesia the Farmers' Association pressed for a monopoly in the home market in maize, wheat, and eggs for Europeans,[4] but failed to secure it. The policy in neighbouring Territories is relevant in Central Africa for the same influences operate, in greater or less degree, from

[1] Hailey, *op. cit.* pp. 740–1.   [2] *Op. cit.* p. 810.
[3] S. T. van der Horst, *Native Labour in South Africa*, pp. 310–11.
[4] W. K. Hancock, *Survey of British Commonwealth Affairs*, Vol. ii, Part ii, pp. 111–12.

the Union to Kenya; and, indeed, there is a strong movement for the amalgamation of Northern Rhodesia and
Nyasaland with Southern Rhodesia.[1] During the war,
when many agricultural products have been short, the
competition for markets has of course eased, but the competition which existed until 1940 may well reappear.

Erosion in African areas is a further cause of opposition
between European and African. The European is concerned
by the threat to the fertility of the whole country, which
deforestation and erosion create, and often condemns
African agriculture for its alleged inefficiency, while the
African blames the European for his shortage of land.

In cattle areas a moral conflict is interwoven with the
economic; for one of the causes of over-stocking is that
Africans value cattle not only for milk, meat, draft, and
breeding, as do Europeans: they value them also as a means
of maintaining good relations with the ancestors, as the most
appropriate form of gifts at marriage, and as a symbol of
wealth and power. For the three latter purposes the quantity of cattle rather than their quality, is important. Europeans insist that cattle *should* be valued only for food,
breeding and draft, and that therefore a reduction of stock
would be profitable. Africans continue to value them for
other purposes.[2]

We believe that the relative value Africans set on cattle
for religious purposes, and for display, has sometimes been
exaggerated, and the economic difficulties in the way of
stock reduction overlooked;[3] nevertheless, the conflict of
values is a real one.

---

[1] Cf. *op. cit.* Chap. i, Section v.

[2] Cf. Margaret Read, *Native Standards of Living and African Culture Change*,
pp. 25–36.

[3] In the Transkei and Ciskei the refusal of Africans to reduce their stock
is usually attributed to their 'non-economic attitude', and the economic
difficulties of reduction are minimized. In fact, since pasture is held in

Most marked in Northern Rhodesia is the conflict over wages in town and on European-owned farms, and over the training of Africans for, and employment in, skilled work. Twice in five years racial tension on the copperbelt has led to riots which necessitated military intervention. In both cases wages were a major grievance. In 1940, African workers also claimed that they were qualified to do the work normally done by Europeans. 'They issued a challenge that they should be so tested by one shift being worked by Europeans and one by Africans, in order to show which shift achieved greater production.'[1] There is no statutory colour bar, but established convention excludes Africans from skilled work on the copper mines and on the railways. A Government Trades School exists in Lusaka, and some of the mission schools give training in carpentry, masonry, printing, etc., but from the main form of technical training —apprenticeship on the mines and railways—Africans are excluded.[2] Authorities in the Government Trades School

common, reduction of stock is only profitable if a whole community reduces its stock. The go-ahead man who bought a few good cows would lose them if he tried to graze them on the common pasture, for they are less hardy than scrub cattle. Agreement to limit is difficult to secure, for either the well-to-do (the men of authority) must suffer most (when the number of cattle per owner which may be grazed is limited), or the poor denied the right to graze cattle at all (if each man is allowed to keep only a proportion of his stock). In spite of these difficulties some districts in the Transkei and Ciskei have agreed to reduction of stock, but to attribute all the opposition to reduction to a 'magical attitude' towards cattle is absurd. We have no first-hand knowledge of over-stocked areas in Central Africa, but suggest that the same difficulties in the way of limitation may operate there, as in the Union.

[1] *Report of the Commission Appointed to Inquire into the Disturbances in the Copperbelt, Northern Rhodesia,* July–Sept. 1935 (T 1089, 10–35). *Report of the Commission Appointed to Inquire into the Disturbances in the Copperbelt, Northern Rhodesia,* July 1940 (E 474, 9–40).

[2] Africans are expressly excluded from the operation of Ordinance 15 of 1943, which regulates the training and employment of apprentices in certain industries and trades. The Employment of Natives Ordinance has never been used for apprenticeship for trades proper. (We are indebted to Mr Saffery, Labour Officer, Ndola, for information on this point.)

are, indeed, careful to point out to visitors that they concentrate on teaching trades in which Africans are not likely to compete with Europeans.

Like most of the rest of the world Central Africa suffered, between the wars, from violent fluctuations in the world market, and a period of 'over-production' and unemployment. As a result of the curtailment of world copper production, for example, Africans employed by mines in Northern Rhodesia fell from 16,726 in 1930 to 6,664 in 1932; Europeans from 1,903 to 1,066. The total paid African labour force fell from about 70,000 to about 54,000.[1]

To ensure a market for their goods producers seek to limit production, and to keep down costs, by paying low wages. The Northern Rhodesian copper-producing companies were members of an international copper cartel, and until the outbreak of war had their quota which they might not exceed. Similarly, the production of tea and coffee in Central Africa was limited by international agreements, and the production of maize in Northern Rhodesia by a maize control board. The economic colour bar is, as we have noted, a further form of restriction of production, for it limits the acquisition of skill, giving the monopoly in certain occupations to a small minority of the community.

But the limitation of production and the depression of wages also limits markets. Thus the struggle over wages and the training and employment of Africans in skilled work, besides being a main issue in racial opposition, is a struggle over the cure for 'over-production' and unemployment—whether it lies in limitation of production, or in the expansion of markets through a rise in the purchasing power of the poorer groups. 'Over-production' and unemployment exacerbate racial opposition by increasing competition for

[1] Report of the Commission on the Financial and Economic Position of Northern Rhodesia. Colonial No. 145, 1938.

markets and jobs. Racial opposition, in turn, facilitates restriction of production by the economic colour bar, and by the insistence that Africans, being totally different from Europeans, do not *need* higher wages than they are getting. Thus racial opposition, and opposition over economic expansion and restriction, are inextricably bound up together.

The disproportion of the population in town and country described in our first chapter (*vide supra*, pp. 17 ff.) is directly related to low wages, and to industrial booms and slumps. Men cannot easily support a wife and three or four children in town—still less elderly relatives—on the wages received for unskilled labour.[1] Further, Government policy in Northern Rhodesia has been directed against the urbanization of Africans because of the difficulties involved during slumps if large numbers of Africans are settled in town.[2]

The disproportionate number of women and children and old people in the country is, in turn, the main cause of hunger there. 'About 110,000 able-bodied and mainly young men have been drawn from the native villages of Northern Rhodesia into non-agricultural work, but no proportionate number of the general population has gone with them; and it is this fact that so severely limits the agricultural market. Had a proportionate number of the general population followed the young able-bodied men, there would now be about 600,000 instead of about 200,000 Northern Rhodesian natives to constitute a market for agricultural produce. Agricultural techniques would have been

[1] Godfrey Wilson, *The Economics of Detribalization in Northern Rhodesia*, Part II, pp. 27–8.

[2] The Government has in fact been loath to admit that urbanization is beginning. In 1938 the Chief Secretary of Northern Rhodesia stated in a speech in Broken Hill that Northern Rhodesia had practically no detribalized natives, yet at that date 69·9 % of the workers of Broken Hill had spent more than two-thirds of their time in town since leaving the country (Godfrey Wilson, *op. cit.* Part I, pp. 42–7), and it was common knowledge among District Officers that urbanization was proceeding.

revolutionized everywhere to meet the new demand, and the rural population would have prospered and begun to increase. As it is, the disproportionate withdrawal of young men has upset the old balance of primitive agriculture, without creating a sufficient new market to revolutionize it, and to give rise to a new equilibrium. The fiancées, some of the wives and children, the infirm relatives, the parents and parents-in-law of the urban labourers, instead of living in town and buying their food—as they would do were world economy more balanced—remain in the country to weight its agriculture down towards inefficiency. Unless they follow the young men to town there can be no general agricultural revolution, for there will be no sufficient market to stimulate it; without an agricultural revolution they must go hungrier than before, for the young men are not there to help them.

'The *chitemene* systems, which obtain over so large a part of Northern Rhodesia, require able-bodied male labour to work them; and their adequacy to feed the rural population is essentially dependent upon the presence of a more or less normal proportion of able-bodied males; female labour can only be substituted for male labour to a very limited degree. The women are occupied in cooking, grinding, pulling branches, etc.; for the cutting and fencing they have neither time nor strength. There is good evidence to suggest that, even before the primitive economy of Northern Rhodesia was disturbed by the immigrant Europeans, there was recurrent hunger; it is certain that the present disproportion of population in many rural areas has increased it. With only about 20 % of the young men under thirty-five to assist them, about 80 % of the rest of the population cannot feed itself as adequately as before, unless agricultural methods are radically changed. There have been slight changes of method; but there has been no agricultural revolution to match the new need. There could not be without such capital investment in the rural areas as cannot, in the absence of a profitable market for produce, possibly be provided.'[1] The fact that labour is migrant, men constantly circulating from town to country and back again, is another factor limiting the development of agricultural skill, and, as we have seen, it may even lead to loss of traditional skills (*vide supra*, p. 19).

Hunger in the country, together with low wages and bad housing in town, are, in their turn, a main cause of the ill-health so general among Africans. Most workers in town have not the money to buy the meat, fish, milk and vegetables which they like as relish to eat with their mainstay, maize or millet; while in the country there is often not enough even of cereals. Ignorance and continuing belief in witchcraft contribute to the ill-health, but inadequate food is the chief factor.

Opposition over beer is likewise related to the disproportion of population—the many lonely men in town drink more than they would were their wives with them—as well as to the racial opposition (*vide supra*, p. 15). The Africans, almost to a man, are opposed to the beer-hall system, and to many the beer laws are simply a form of European oppression to be evaded whenever possible. The Europeans, for their part, insist that home brewing, which the majority of Africans want, involves widespread drunkenness and disorder. Constantly fearing lest 'the natives get out of hand', Europeans are much concerned by African over-drinking. Thus a simple opposition over licensing laws is so exacerbated by the underlying radical opposition as to become uncontrollable. The statutory beer laws in the urban areas of Northern Rhodesia cannot, in fact, be enforced.

[1] Godfrey Wilson, *op. cit.* Part 1, pp. 50–1.

Not only does disproportion of population make for hunger, ill-health and drunkenness; it also, as we have seen, makes stable marriage among Africans practically impossible (*vide supra*, pp. 22–3). At every point, indeed, economic and moral issues are intertwined. The economic conflict over land and markets and skilled jobs is at the same time a moral conflict over race. Shall race be a ground of economic distinction or not? This appears within the Church as conflict between those who wish to exclude Africans from the buildings in which Europeans worship, and those who insist that such an exclusion is a denial of the 'Fellowship of the Holy Ghost', which is prayed for by every Christian congregation.

There is a further conflict between the values of so-called 'racial purity' and sexual satisfaction. Extra-marital relations between European and African are not illegal in Central Africa as they are in the Union, but there is strong moral pressure against them in a section of the community. Nevertheless, miscegenation is common. Indeed, competition between European and African men for African women is an important cause of racial tension in the mining areas.[1] The fact that European men can afford to offer more than Africans exacerbates the situation.

As we have already noted (*vide supra*, p. 15) there is acute opposition over witchcraft, and this again is entangled with the opposition over race; for the Africans as a group mostly believe in the power of witchcraft, the Europeans[2] mostly do not. Europeans seek to enforce a law making imputation of witchcraft a punishable offence, and Africans seek to

[1] Godfrey Wilson, *op. cit.* Part II, p. 66.

[2] Acquaintance with the gossip of country districts in the Union, and a study of the Union and Southern Rhodesian press, shows that an appreciable number of Europeans have absorbed African magical concepts, and patronize African magical practitioners. The same is probably true of some Europeans in Central Africa, but we have no direct evidence on them.

evade it. Europeans ridicule Africans for their belief and cite it as proof of low mental ability. Africans, for their part, think the Europeans either ignorant or hypocritical. Often we have heard it said of someone whose illness was believed to be caused by the ancestors or by witches: 'It is of no use going with her to a European doctor; this is a disease Europeans do not understand.' And this among people who would willingly go to a European doctor in certain cases. More than one African friend also has reproached us with concealing our real beliefs: 'Of course people among you work witchcraft, and you have medicines for protection, only you won't admit it. Why won't you admit it to me? I have told you what we believe.' To some Africans the European law against the imputation of witchcraft is the cause of increasing ill-health.[1]

There is contradiction also between African and European over race (*vide supra*, p. 16), and argument within the European group itself between those who believe that the African is intellectually incapable of civilization, and those who believe that he is potentially as capable as any other group. The racial argument, in its more scientific form, is an assertion of racial differences in the size, type and rate of growth of the brain, and of a correlated difference in mental capacity. Racialists point also to differences in the scores of different races in intelligence tests. The non-racialists reply that no relation between the size of brain and mental capacity has been proved, and that the so-called 'primitiveness' of structure in some non-European brains may allow of greater advance than the more specialized 'superior' types. They insist that the scores in all intelligence tests so far devised are affected by environment, and so are no true criterion of racial capacity, the tests in which Europeans score high being those set by Europeans with

[1] Cf. Hunter, *op. cit.* p. 275.

their own background in mind.[1] They point also to the great intellectual achievements of Africans who have opportunities of education.

So, too, there is argument between those who believe that Africans are children of Ham, predestined to be hewers of wood and drawers of water, and those who believe that all men were born brothers. The doctrine of a Herrenvolk is preached by British Israelites and others, and flatly contradicts the doctrines of democracy.

Disharmony between the races finds expression in mutual rudeness (*vide supra*, p. 15) and extreme incompatibility of taste. To many Europeans, Africans in European dress are ugly or ridiculous, and the skill of the more sophisticated in European dances is distasteful. They hanker after the romance of the primitive: it is in beads and barkcloth, dancing traditional dances, that the African attracts them. To the racialist it is not appropriate that an African should look like a European in any way. Many Africans, on their part, delight in European dress and dances, finding in them one of the few means available to them of expressing their claim to be civilized men.[2]

The general level of knowledge and skill in Central Africa is in some respects inadequate to the range of relations. Tension between Africans and Europeans is exacerbated by ignorance of each other's languages and conventions. The greater harmony between employer and employee, when one can speak the language of the other, is very marked. Deliberate rudeness occurs often enough, but added to that is disharmony created by Europeans, in their ignorance, paying directly for gifts offered by Africans, or failing to make the expected return gift; by Africans asking gifts of Europeans as they would from a chief, and being treated as

---

[1] Cf. S. Biesheuvel, *African Intelligence*.
[2] Cf. Godfrey Wilson, *op. cit.* Part II, pp. 18–19.

importunate beggars; by the African visitor waiting, as seems only polite to him, to be asked his business, and by the European waiting impatiently for him to state it.

By civilized standards the Africans as a group are both ignorant and unskilful. Again, this maladjustment is related both to the racial opposition and to the opposition between restriction and expansion. The racialists argue that the African is incapable of benefiting by any save the most elementary school education, and many argue that even learning to read and to write 'spoils the native'. Restrictionist forces, as we have seen, oppose education for Africans on the ground that production, and therefore the numbers trained for skilled jobs, must be limited.

Finally, Central Africa is involved in the present war. This violent opposition is bound up with the oppositions apparent within Central Africa itself. It is, in one aspect, an opposition over race. The Nazi dogma of race is essentially the same as that maintained by the majority of Europeans in Central Africa; the non-racial dogmas preached, albeit inconsistently (*vide infra*, p. 151) by the Allies, are those preached, also inconsistently, in Central Africa. Regarded from another angle the war is a product of 'over-production' and unemployment. It was in the misery of the German slump that the Nazi party bred, and competition for markets contributed to the opposition both with Germany and with Japan.

We argue then that the oppositions and maladjustments which mark Central African society are essentially one. Racial opposition is bound up with the opposition over expansion or restriction of production. The disproportion of the sexes in town and country, hunger in the villages, African ill-health, and the instability of marriage are concomitants of these oppositions, each depending upon the others. Opposition over witchcraft both exacerbates and is exacerbated by the racial opposition. Ordinary oppositions such as competition for land, conflict over licensing laws, quarrels between husbands and wives, are immensely aggravated by the underlying radical opposition. The issues of the present war are closely related to the opposition within Central Africa itself.

The underlying opposition is an opposition over scale. The racial opposition is an opposition over the range of religious inclusiveness—over the value, significance and beauty of relations with non-Europeans or, in the case of Germany, with non-'Aryans'. Colour bars in education and industry limit the development of human resources and so limit wealth, knowledge, and skill, that is, control of the material environment. So also the opposition over wages is an opposition over the limitation or expansion of material scale. Expansion of consumption through a rise in the standard of living, and corresponding expansion of production, is an increase in scale: depression of wages and limitation of production is a limitation of scale. The opposition over witchcraft is a struggle between more and less magical forms of religion—again an opposition between narrower and wider scale forms.

Generally speaking the range and intensity of material relations has outrun religious inclusiveness, hence racial opposition, international war, and violent economic fluctuations. There can be no subordination in the wider relations, such as is necessary to control fluctuations in the world market and international war, unless these wider relations are intrinsically valued by the parties to them, that is, by us all.

This outrunning of the religious aspect of relations by the material also appears as the combination of non-complementary with complementary diversity. European and African, German and British are in close relations because they work and trade together, but racial and non-racial religions are contradictory, rather than complementary. Only when different religions are mutually tolerant—when, for example, neither Christian nor communist believes the other to be necessarily damned—are they complementary. Similarly, the necessity for a planned economy, if economic fluctuations are to be overcome, is the necessity for securing that economic differentiation be complementary; that, for example, copper production be organized in the interests of the whole community, not only in the interests of a small group of shareholders, or of the European skilled workers alone. Specialization and variety, as opposed to non-complementary diversity, imply some community of value, dogma and aesthetic intuition (*vide supra*, pp. 84–5).

Although the material aspect has generally outrun the religious in our society, there are particular cases when religious change has outrun the material. Certain Nyakyusa who have accepted monogamy, but have not yet made the necessary economic adjustments, have already been mentioned (*vide supra*, p. 126). Polygyny, we argue, involves a subordinate position for women. When the status or women *vis-à-vis* men is low, their activities are circumscribed; their mobility is limited. The change from polygyny to monogamy, by giving women a more equal status with men, tends towards greater mobility, and is thus an increase in scale. We are aware that some very primitive peoples are monogamous—they are usually also without a caste system—nevertheless, limitations of mobility by caste and sex are, in themselves, limitations of scale (*vide supra*, Chapter IV (*e*)).

Within the material aspect production has outrun consumption, hence unemployment; industrial development has outrun agricultural development, hence hunger in the reserves and ill-health; economic co-operation has outrun the learning of each other's manners and languages, thus increasing tension between employer and employee.

The unity of the particular oppositions and maladjustments evident in Central Africa, the fact that they are all manifestations of an underlying opposition over scale is not, however, and cannot be, generally realized. Superficially the racial conflict appears to be, in its economic aspect, an ordinary competition for wealth and position. To the majority of Europeans involved it is a question of whether they or Africans shall have the good jobs and land and markets. Only by some is it seen that the racial struggle is inextricably bound up with the world conflict over the expansion and restriction of production; that the conflict is *both* over wages and over markets. Employers want markets but limit them by limiting wages; the skilled Europeans want jobs, but through colour-bar restrictions they also restrict the market, and so the jobs available. Those who press for low wages and colour bar hope of course to keep their cake and eat the other fellow's by selling their goods elsewhere; but they cannot do this indefinitely. It is beginning to be admitted in the Union that the development of secondary industries in the Union depends upon the development of the African market, but by some the market is still hopefully pushed into 'neighbouring Territories', thus obscuring the necessary implication that African wages must rise before the market can expand.[1]

The opposition is muddled at every point. The same people complain that African agriculture is inefficient, but at the same time fear African competition in agricultural produce, and therefore oppose the development of tribal areas. The same people want skilled, English-speaking

[1] The fact that African wages within the Union must rise if secondary industries are to flourish is clearly recognized in the *Third Interim Report of the Industrial and Agricultural Requirements Commission*, U.G. 40–41.

servants, and hygienic locations, while simultaneously they oppose school education for Africans, and grudge the money necessary for adequate houses and water and sanitation. The same people mourn the disappearance of primitive dress and dances, while simultaneously they expect to have African labourers in town and a market for civilized goods. The same people preach the brotherhood of man, but shrink from social intercourse with Africans, and are horrified at miscegenation. Africans seek education and recognition as civilized men, but they cling to belief in witchcraft.

Similar contradictions are apparent in the present war. The Allies oppose the Nazi dogma of race, yet most of the Europeans in Central Africa, while supporting the Allied cause, do not accept the implications of non-racialism. Even in England itself there is argument whether the Atlantic Charter shall apply to all races or not. Again, the Allies profess to be fighting both for the restoration of national sovereignty, and for freedom from want for the common man. Now freedom from want implies a rise in the general standard of living which is dependent upon an increase in the scale of material relations; it also implies control of slumps. None of these is possible without a high degree of subordination in the wider relations—without effective international planning—yet national sovereignty is a denial of subordination in the wider relations. England went to war with Germany in support *both* of the political and economic disunity of Europe which Germany wished to unify, *and* of a relatively high degree of individual and sectional autonomy within political unities, an autonomy that Germany sought to minimize. Actually European unity goes with a high degree of individual and sectional autonomy and European disunity with a low degree (*vide supra*, pp. 108–15). That this is not understood is part of the disequilibrium. For the contradictions to be generally realized is for them to be resolved.

When opposition is muddled social pressure operates in opposite directions and men are forced into illegality, illogicality and unconventionality. Their behaviour is necessarily somewhat inefficient and immoral, inaccurate and heretical, unskilful and ugly. If, for example, an African believes that his child has died of witchcraft he is compelled to take steps against the supposed witch, yet if he does so he may be prosecuted. Similarly, a European pastor with African and European parishioners, cannot, even if he wishes to do so, have easy social relations with both groups. If he invite Africans to his house the Europeans will feel that he is 'letting down the prestige of the white man'; if he fails to entertain Africans some of them at least will think him a hypocrite. He is forced into behaviour which half his congregation finds immoral. We have already mentioned the difficulties of Nyakyusa Christians in being both hospitable and monogamous (*vide supra*, p. 126). Bemba in Broken Hill are in a similar quandary: if they carry out their traditional marriage ceremonies members of other tribes laugh at them; if they do not perform the ceremonies their relatives in the villages deride them on their return there. They cannot keep the conventions of both country and town, and they circulate from one to the other.

The conflict of loyalties in the present war is very obvious. The military alinement is on national lines, but within each state there is opposition between Fascism and Democracy, between narrow- and wide-scale tendencies. For the Democrat in Axis countries there is conflict between national patriotism and the values of democracy; for the Fascist in Allied countries there is similar conflict. Hence the emergence of a 'Fifth Column' in almost every country, and the spectacle of one national state after another changing sides.

These are examples of the most crude oppositions of law, of logic, and of convention, which only press on certain groups in our society; but, we maintain, social pressure operates in opposite ways on everyone in our society. In so far as there is muddle there is conflict of law, contradiction of logical limitations, and disharmony of conventions in all relations.

The oppositions and maladjustments of Central Africa are, in fact, intolerable, and are compelling change. There are already tendencies towards the reduction of the disproportion of population in town and country, more women and dependents beginning to accompany the young men to town.[1] Erosion, hunger in the reserves, and the poor health of the Africans are not accepted as unavoidable inefficiencies. They are intolerable because the knowledge and skill and capital to overcome them exist. Recurrent famine and uncontrolled malarial infection may be necessary evils in a primitive society which has not the means to overcome them; but in our large-scale society the failure to overcome them is found both inefficient and immoral. Among the expressed objects of the Colonial Development Fund is the control of erosion and the improvement of nutrition and health.

The ignorance and unskilfulness of Africans in civilization is likewise intolerable. The storekeeper is furious at the 'stupidity' of his delivery boy who delivers parcels to the wrong addresses because he cannot read, and though he may disapprove of schooling for Africans in principle, he engages literates himself. The housewife is equally irritated by the incompetence of an untrained cook, and demands proper training schools for domestic servants. Neither

[1] Godfrey Wilson, *op. cit.* Part i, p. 36.

accept the low standard of knowledge and skill as a necessary evil. The Africans themselves are constantly pressing for more education, particularly for teaching in English, and schools did in fact develop considerably in Central Africa between 1930 and 1940.

'Over-production', unemployment and violent fluctuations in the world market compel men to find ways of overcoming them. Social security schemes, plans for currency control, and attempts to nationalize the means of production are symptoms of profound dissatisfaction with these inefficiencies. The international anarchy presses on states, however reluctant, the necessity of accepting some limitation of national sovereignty.

Less obvious to the European observer are the attempts made by Africans to reinterpret the traditional magical beliefs so that they may be more compatible with European ideas. Nyakyusa who have been to school lay more stress on sorcery than on witchcraft, some teachers even insisting that they do not believe in witchcraft at all, but only in sorcery.[1] Now sorcery (*ubutege*) includes poisoning, and these teachers are very vague in their own minds about the line between sorcery which involves putting poison in one's enemy's food, and sorcery which involves burying a charm under his doorway, or in the thatch of his hut. They translate *ubutege* to themselves as 'poisoning' and find it quite compatible with their training in hygiene.

These changes are all manifestations of the tendency of the scale of society to even up, that is, of the tendency towards equilibrium. Agricultural development to match the industrial development is beginning to be planned: the gap between the increase in the African's economic range (through his participation in industry) and his knowledge

[1] For an outline of Nyakyusa religious beliefs see Godfrey Wilson, 'An African morality', *Africa*, Jan. 1936.

and skill, is somewhat reduced: some subordination in the wider relations to match the range of economic relations is attempted. In BuNyakyusa we could trace tendencies towards an increase in economic scale, through specialization, to match the religious expansion appearing in the acceptance of monogamy. The scientific element in the belief in death through the machinations of one's enemies— poisoning—is emphasized at the expense of the magical elements, thus slightly narrowing the gap between the wide-scale science taught by Europeans and the smaller scale religion of the African.

Nevertheless, the scale of Central African society is getting more and more uneven, for primary change—increase of scale in the material aspect—is proceeding faster than secondary adjustments are made. The range and intensity of material relations continues to increase faster than does religious inclusiveness. More and more Africans are being drawn into industry in Central Africa, and both town and country dwellers are becoming more and more dependent upon foreign goods. The intensity of relations between European and African is thereby increased, but there is no comparable increase in religious inclusiveness. Racial opposition is much more acute in the mining towns than in the villages, and as the proportion of Africans in town increases opposition in Central Africa as a whole increases. It is on the semi-skilled man in town that colour bar in industry presses, not on his brother in the country; it is the economically most civilized—those most dependent upon wages or on cash crops—who are worst hit by slumps.

During the period between the wars the conflict of values in the Union has resulted in the defeat of the policy of 'equal rights for all civilized men' and the triumph of the policy of racial discrimination, which has been incorporated in successive Acts.[1] Union policy reacts on Central African policy—many of the Europeans in Central Africa are South African by birth and sympathy—and the entrenchment of a caste system in the Union fortifies racialism in Central Africa, tending to prevent any increase in racial inclusiveness there also.

In the world as a whole, markets were not expanding as fast as production: the development of scientific knowledge and of techniques far outran sympathy for and understanding of foreigners. Although communications were enormously speeded up and international trade and scientific and technical interchange were extending, still the value of national sovereignty was maintained.

Efforts have been made to limit the scale of relations in the material aspect in which they are widest. Destruction of crops, quotas for agricultural and industrial production, and the suppression of new techniques by the buying up and smothering of patents, are all devices to limit economic and technical relations, and they were widely employed before 1939.[2] There is limitation of scientific research also in countries other than Nazi Germany: it is very difficult, for example, for a social scientist to get access to the mine compounds of Northern Rhodesia, and anthropological research in the reserves of the Union of South Africa is similarly hampered.

Such limitations of material expansion are, however, sporadic, and are widely regarded as immoral, since they are contrary to the current value of 'progress', i.e. of

[1] E.g. 1923 Natives (Urban Areas) Act; 1926 Mines and Works Act 1911 Amendment Act (Colour Bar Act); 1926 Masters and Servants Law Amendment Act; 1926 'Immorality' Act; 1930 Riotous Assemblies (Amendment) Act; 1930 Natives (Urban Areas) Act 1923 Amendment Act; 1932 Native Service Contract Act; 1936 Representation of the Natives Act. For a brilliant account of the Union situation see R. F. A. Hoernlé, *South African Native Policy and the Liberal Spirit*, 1939.

[2] Cf. L. Robbins, *The Economic Basis of the Class Conflict.*

material expansion. Thus, in spite of restrictionist tendencies, increase in material scale continues faster than does increase in religious scale. Disequilibrium is growing.

As we have already noted, opposition and maladjustment are more acute in some areas of Central Africa than in others. Racial opposition is intense in the mining areas, but is relatively slight in remote BuNyakyusa. Competition for land, erosion, disproportion of population, and hunger affect some rural areas much more than others. Nevertheless, disequilibrium is integral and the oppositions and maladjustments of each area react on the others. Racial opposition in the mining towns breeds racial opposition in the villages. Hunger in the country drives more and more Africans into industry, thereby tending to depress town wages. Low wages in turn limit the market for agricultural produce and retard the development of the country.

Not only, however, is the degree of disequilibrium in one district dependent upon the degree in others within Central Africa; it is dependent upon the degree of disequilibrium in the world as a whole. The unevenness between the range of material and religious relations, between production and consumption, between agriculture and industry are world phenomena. The overcoming of racial opposition and international war, of over-production and unemployment, of hunger and ill-health, depend upon their resolution or increase in the world as a whole. There is a measure of local autonomy, but it is relative, not absolute. Thus the muddled oppositions we describe in Central Africa are but one local manifestation of the blind and contradictory strivings of our world.

CHAPTER VI

PRACTICAL IMPLICATIONS

(a) THE IMPLICATIONS OF EXPANSION IN SCALE

FIRST, then, we argue: the change from primitive to civilized necessarily involves certain specific social changes. The increase in scale implies not only a greater range of material relations, but also a wider religious inclusiveness. It implies not only greater specialization and greater control of the material environment, but also greater religious variety, and a less magical religion. It implies the greater importance of impersonal relations and greater mobility; its structural form is the combination of greater autonomy in the narrower relations with subordination in the wider. These are characteristics of the historical as well as of the contemporary moment.

There is a degree of autonomy between the cultural characteristics of scale, but it is only relative: religious exclusiveness limits the range of material relations; if there is little specialization there can be no great control of the material environment; if there is little mobility, the use of human resources and therefore control of the material environment is limited; if there is no religious variety, or if relations are largely personal, religion is necessarily magical; if religion is magical, control of the environment is limited.

In concrete terms this implies, in Central Africa, that there must inevitably be an increase in religious range along with the increase in the range of material relations. The traditional parochial religions are incompatible with expanding trade and travel. So long as foreigners are regarded as dangerous enemies to whom one has no obligations, trade or other co-operation with them is impossible. A modicum of law and order are a condition of trade,[1] and law depends upon inclusiveness of value. It is nothing but the form of material and religious intensity, the pressure men exert on one another.

The relative autonomy between the material and religious aspects of relations is typified in the attitude of Europeans towards trade with Indians in Northern Rhodesia. 'Business is business', and many Europeans deal with Indians, yet they feel it necessary to defend their action before other Europeans. 'I don't care, I shop at the Sammies (Indians). They are so *much* cheaper. X & X (European firms) put on the price ridiculously' was a typical remark heard at a tea party in Northern Rhodesia. The speaker was a Natal-born European. Religion in Northern Rhodesia is sufficiently inclusive for Indian immigrants to be admitted, and their property rights protected, so trade with them is possible, but race feeling considerably restricts that trade. We know of Europeans transferring their custom from Indians to fellow-Europeans on the ground of race alone, and efforts have been made by certain Europeans to restrict the trading rights of Indians.

Greater specialization is a condition of increasing control of the Central African environment. Increase in production, for instance, depends, among other things, on specializing industrial and agricultural labour, that is, on stabilization of the labour force. So long as there is migrant labour neither skill in agricultural work, nor skill in industry, can develop far. As we have seen, the Bemba complain that the present generation of migrant labourers are less skilled in agriculture than their peasant fathers. An agricultural officer in the Union told us of similar difficulties. His work, he said, was stultified because the villagers repeatedly left

[1] Cf. W. K. Hancock, *op. cit.* Vol. II, Part II, pp. 162–8.

to work in town just as they were beginning to learn better agricultural methods. They never remained in the country long enough to acquire and apply greater skill. At the same time the unskilfulness of the African in industry is the subject of unceasing complaint among Europeans.[1] Specialization and the development of skill in industry is further limited by the rapid circulation of Africans from job to job, in town.[2]

Some argue that in a highly organized industry only a small proportion of skilled workers is necessary, the majority being engaged in repetitive, relatively unskilled work. It is observable, however, that when maximum production is required (as in war-time) the demand for skilled specialists is unlimited. In so far as the racial barrier is rigidly maintained in Central Africa control of the environment is limited. Colour, not capacity, is the main criterion of fitness for technical and professional training, and employment, so that human resources are not fully used.

In the increase of specialization is involved the decay of traditional handicrafts. Primitive techniques of iron smelting and of weaving, for example, cannot compete against the products of specialized industries. Already in Central Africa machine-made hoes and cloth are more

[1] It would be interesting to compare the level of skill among Africans in the Union Minière, Belgian Congo, which has aimed at a stabilized labour force, with that on the copperbelt of Northern Rhodesia, where there is more migrant labour. Unfortunately, we were not able to study this as we had planned to do.

[2] Godfrey Wilson, *The Economics of Detribalization*, Part I, pp. 56–7. Cf. S. H. Frankel, *op. cit.* p. 145. Mr J. D. F. Briggs, speaking at a conference of the South African Trades and Labour Council said: 'In other countries the unskilled worker remained in one industry and developed a certain measure of skill. In South Africa, Natives drifted from one industry to another and learned nothing. As a bricklayer he needed four Natives to keep him going when he was working hard. In Australia one labourer kept two bricklayers busy, because he knew his job.' Reported *Daily Despatch*, East London, 30 April 1943.

commonly used than local products. Where village industries survive, as in the weaving of the west coast of Africa,
and in India, the traditional skill is relatively great, and as
the standard of living of the village craftsman is so much
lower than that of industrialized groups he can still compete with them.

Schools are a necessary specialization in a civilized
society, because the quantity of knowledge and elaboration
of skill necessary to a civilized man is great. The primitive system of education through participation in adult
activities[1] is adequate only when the knowledge to be
acquired is not very great, and the skills are relatively
simple. It cannot alone suffice in a civilized society, though
in the form of apprenticeship it remains an important part
of the civilized educational system.

Religious variety, including aesthetic variety, is, like
specialization, an integral part of a civilized society. It is
not merely a temporary phenomenon of the change from
primitive to civilized. Local differences in art tend to
disappear as groups become less isolated, just as local
differences in law, morality and economic organization, in
logic, science and dogma, in convention and technique
disappear; but society is not thereby made uniform.
Civilized art far surpasses that of any primitive society in
its rich diversity. Variety will remain as Central Africa
becomes more civilized, but not all the religious differences
we have noted there are complementary. The non-complementary differences cannot be maintained. It is only in so
far as the different religions are tolerant of one another that
they can maintain themselves in their present form.

The traditional religions are incompatible with modern
Central African society, not only because they admit of so

[1] Cf. M. Fortes, 'Social and psychological aspects of education in Tale-
land', 1938 (Supplement to *Africa*, Vol. XI, No. 4).

little diversity within the community, and are parochial, but also because they are so magical. A decline in magicality is one of the conditions of increase in knowledge and skill—particularly of improved hygiene, and control of erosion. Decline in magicality is, in its turn, dependent upon the increasing impersonality of relations. Belief in witchcraft and magic, and the predominance of personal relations are correlated. When the harshness of impersonal relations is criticized, the connection between increasing impersonality and the decline of belief in witchcraft is usually overlooked.

Granted the economic and religious changes which have taken place in Central Africa, centralization, involving loss of relative power by petty chiefs and kinsmen, is inevitable. When people cease to live in kinship groups many of the legal functions of kinsmen must be taken over by courts with a wider jurisdiction. For example, in Broken Hill, kinsmen cannot by themselves enforce the traditional Bemba marriage law, because their young relatives are no longer dependent upon them economically or religiously.[1] Any attempt to bolster up a legal system based on kinship is doomed to failure in an expanding society, for it is part of a small-scale system. Wide-scale law is a necessary part of a wide-scale society. So also African thought and forms of expression must be subordinated to the logic and conventions of our wide-scale society. Any attempt to keep African art 'uncontaminated' by European tradition and conventions is futile. This does not, however, preclude the development of African 'schools' in music and dancing and sculpture, for centralization does not imply the loss of freedom. Within the centralized system there must be a high degree of individual and local autonomy. Without this there cannot be specialization and variety, or mobility. The specialized knowledge and skill of the doctor, the agricul-

[1] Godfrey Wilson, *op. cit.* Part II, pp. 39–63.

tural demonstrator, or the teacher cannot be exercised unless they have freedom. So, too, the specialized knowledge of local conditions which a chief, a District Officer, or a Territorial administration and Legislative Council may have, is useless, unless they have a degree of autonomy. Freedom of conscience, freedom of artistic expression, freedom to choose one's friends and associates are, we maintain, essential characteristics of a large-scale society. Without them scale is limited (*vide supra*, pp. 108–15).

The implication of expansion in historical scale is that Central African society is becoming more flexible. As men become less magical the particular forms of behaviour followed by their fathers no longer seem to them the only good and possible way. Thus, the 'conservatism of the African' on which Europeans often dwell, is daily diminishing, as the scale of their society expands. Expansion in historical scale does not imply cutting adrift from the past— the radical who ignores history is no less small scale in outlook than the conservative who resists all change—but it does imply a relative freedom from the immediate and parochial past. It is in the realization of himself as heir to centuries of civilization that the African becomes adaptable, not in dwelling on the parochial doings of his immediate ancestors.

(b) The Implications of Unevenness in Scale

Our second proposition is that in so far as the characteristics of civilized society are not developing in proportion to one another, there is radical opposition and maladjustment. Incoherence between the correlates of scale is one of the manifestations of disequilibrium. The opposition between European and African is due partly to the fact that the range of material relations has increased without a corresponding increase in religious inclusiveness. Economically, Europeans and Africans are closely dependent on one another; but the majority of Europeans do not value close relations with Africans in any other form. Intermarriage is anathema; educated Africans and those who have adopted European dress and manners are regarded with suspicion. The number of Africans in European employment is steadily increasing, yet it is still insisted that Africans 'must develop on their own lines'. Segregation is the attempt to keep relations between black and white tenuous in all except the economic sphere. It is the most glaring example of unevenness of scale in Africa.

Central Africa, like the rest of the world, is suffering also because the intensity of material relations between nations has increased without a corresponding extension of religious inclusiveness. Until 1939, Britain traded with Germany and eagerly studied her science and technique, but both groups valued national sovereignty more than international co-operation. National interests (so-called) came first and 'cosmopolitan idealists' were despised. Consequently international law remained weak: it was only enforceable in so far as values were inclusive. Even within national states and racial groups values are not consistently inclusive. Sectional interests of class and industry have not been adequately controlled, for they remain, in some degree, non-complementary. The subordination of big business to the common welfare is essentially the same problem as the establishment of international law. It depends upon inclusiveness of value.[1]

The combination of religious inclusiveness with impersonality is difficult. It is easier to imagine a group of foreigners to be all devils, when one does not meet them individually but only trades with them through an imper-

[1] Cf. E. H. Carr, *Conditions of Peace*, Chap. v.

sonally organized corporation, than it is to treat neighbours, with whom one has many-sided relations, as uniformly bad. It is easier for an employer to ignore the hunger of an employee whom he never meets face to face than to ignore the hunger of one he meets daily. Only if there be a high degree of mobility between groups can the relative detachment, born of impersonal relations, be combined with a wide inclusiveness. The man who has travelled and made friends in both England and Germany, among Africans and Europeans, who has been both an employer and an employee, can neither regard the universe in purely personal terms, nor be narrow in his sympathies. It is the lack of mobility between the racial groups in Central Africa which prevents men being both impersonal and inclusive.

Disequilibrium is also manifested as unevenness of scale within each of the correlates of scale. Industry in Central Africa is more specialized than agriculture, hence the poverty of many country districts. Specialist farmers to feed the families of specialist mine labourers are lacking. In many areas it is difficult for Africans to buy the food of the country even when they have money to spend on it. Production and consumption have developed unevenly, hence the danger of recurrent slumps, and the consequent difficulty in establishing a permanent African population in towns. The inefficiency, ignorance, and lack of skill of Africans in agriculture and hygiene is deplored, yet their opportunity of technical and general education, and of doing skilled work, is circumscribed. Europeans are magical about race but not about disease, hence constant quarrels over hygiene in the African quarters of European towns. The danger of unhealthy locations is recognized, but Europeans grudge Africans the money and education which would make healthy locations possible. There is some mobility of labour, but conventional and intellectual exclusiveness. Europeans want Africans in town as labourers but they must remain 'segregated' and 'develop on their own lines'.

We argue that the oppositions and maladjustments of Central Africa are all related, and that none can be resolved without the others. Unemployment and racialism are interdependent; hunger in the country and the instability of marriage are correlated with the disproportion of the sexes in both town and country, which in turn is correlated with low wages and the danger of slumps, which is correlated with uneven development of production and consumption, which, in its turn, is correlated with too little religious inclusiveness for the degree of material intensity (*vide supra*, pp. 136–49). Each opposition reinforces the others. The statesman who seeks to remedy one manifestation of disequilibrium is always in the position of the old woman in the nursery rhyme who could not get her pig over the stile until she found a dog to bite it, could not get the help of the dog until she had found a stick to beat it, and so *ad infinitum*.

The fact that all these oppositions and maladjustments are related and radical is not, however, generally realized. To many the opposition between European and African appears as a competition for places—a struggle for the better paid and more interesting jobs, for political control, for positions of honour and authority. They do not realize it to be the opposition over scale which it is. At every point there is muddle, the same people exerting pressure in opposite directions. The same people employ Africans in European towns, yet seek segregation; the same people demand skilled, English-speaking servants, but oppose education for Africans; the same people preach the brotherhood of man but never invite Africans as guests to their homes.

Disequilibrium is not inevitable in the change from primitive to civilized—a moving equilibrium is possible—but a degree of disequilibrium is unavoidable if the change from primitive to civilized be very rapid. For example, a young Nyakyusa friend of ours, Angombwike, was working outside his home district. He was a Christian, and met a girl of another tribe who attracted him, at Church. He wished to marry her. The Elders of the Church approved, but Angombwike's father refused his consent on the ground that the girl's home was too far from his. Now Angombwike's father was a middle-aged man; he had grown up when travel between chiefdoms was still dangerous, and the difficulties involved in taking a wife from a distance had been impressed on him. When he was young, visits home for Angombwike's sweetheart would have been difficult; she might have been raped on the road; the gifts she brought back might have been stolen before she reached her husband's house. In vain Angombwike protested that times had changed and that nowadays she would travel home safely by lorry. His father's ideas about what marriages were suitable, and what were not, had been formed when distant marriages were in fact unwise. It was difficult for him to share Angombwike's point of view.

In the same way, young Bemba in Broken Hill find it very difficult to support their elderly relatives (as by traditional custom they should do), yet the old people grew up in a society in which it was impossible themselves to make provision for old age. The conditions which make saving possible did not exist for them. Similarly, their knowledge and wisdom is out of date, but they could not have acquired knowledge and wisdom applicable to the present. Schools were not available in their youth, and their experience is mainly applicable to a different form of society.

Because very rapid change in a primitive society necessarily involves opposition and maladjustment of this kind it is often urged that in Africa change should be gradual. But, as we have already pointed out, opposition and maladjustment can only be avoided if *all* the changes are gradual. If, for example, mining develops rapidly, disequilibrium is increased, not avoided, when religious, political and educational change is retarded. The advocates of gradual development seldom conceive of slowing down economic change. So long as rapid change in some aspects continues, disequilibrium can only be diminished if the young radicals can carry the older generation with them. Here the value of adult education is obvious. Some of the Elders concerned in Angombwike's marriage were of the generation of his father, but they had absorbed modern ideas.

Another means of easing rapid change is by the teaching of history. Historical perspective, we have argued, makes a society more adaptable. History, therefore, is not an 'unpractical' and unnecessary subject for Central African schools, and some knowledge and sense of it among the African villagers and European immigrants will, we believe, not only make the conservatives less bound by their immediate past, but the radicals less scornful of tradition, thereby diminishing the opposition between them. If it is to fulfil this function, however, the history taught must not be merely tales of heroes and of wars,[1] but an objective study of the diversity and development of society. If the emphasis be on an immediate and parochial past it will be exclusiveness and conservatism that is fostered, rather than that awareness of the unity and continuity of civilization which breeds adaptability.

[1] In a reputable South African school (with a number of Rhodesian pupils) at which one of the authors was educated, the only references made in history lessons to Africans was in the study of the 'Kaffir wars'. These were studied in detail, battle by battle. The syllabus was that laid down by the 'Joint Matriculation Board' of the Union of South Africa.

(c) THE IMPLICATIONS OF CHOICE IN CENTRAL AFRICA

Our third proposition is that disequilibrium is at present increasing in Central Africa, but that it cannot continue to do so indefinitely. We cannot muddle on with increasing education for Africans and at the same time maintain colour-bar restrictions; we cannot indefinitely increase production and yet leave Africans so poor that they cannot buy the goods produced; we cannot develop international trade and communications and at the same time maintain the absolute sovereignty of national states. Such inconsistencies eventually frustrate themselves. Education is limited when men cannot apply their knowledge and skill; industry comes to a standstill for lack of a market; trade is impossible in international anarchy. Whether we will or no, material expansion must in time stop, unless our religious inclusiveness increases.

Disequilibrium can only diminish with a policy of consistent racialism or non-racialism, with consistent restrictionism or consistent expansionism, with consistent nationalism or internationalism; that is, either by contraction of scale in some respects, or by expansion of scale in others.

Racialism involves a limitation of control of the material environment by limiting our use of resources. The potential skill and intelligence of Africans cannot be exploited so long as skilled jobs are reserved for Europeans. The scientific discoveries of Carver, for example, might not yet have been made, had education been denied coloured people in the United States. Increasing control of the material environment, often called 'progress', is a fundamental value of our society, and racialism involves at least a partial abandonment of it. The hope of conquering poverty and disease must be sacrificed on the altar of race.

Racialism involves economic restrictionism not only because it limits the use of African skill in production, but also because unrestricted production would necessitate the exploitation of the African market, and if Africans are to buy goods they must have both the money and the desire to do so. Only a civilized man is of substantial use as a market. This was early realized in the old Cape Colony when the Government fostered the 'civilization of the Kaffirs for the benefit of trade'. To-day it is noticeable that almost the only illustrations picturing Africans as civilized, which appear in the South African press, are those advertising goods for sale to Africans. The vernacular papers are full of advertisements, inserted by European firms, displaying Africans in elegant European dress, enjoying tea, or using shoe polish, or sitting in easy chairs. With modern methods of production the slave state is not profitable. A reduction in turn-over means higher costs of production, and, except during war, Africans as well as Poles are needed as a market. Thus racialism must be paid for by a lowering of the European standard of living. Its price is the boots and butter, refrigerators and motor-cars of the European.

Racialism excludes skilled service by Africans—the European employer who demands a knowledge of English or literacy is, if he be a racialist, increasing the opposition to his way of life, for as Africans gain in knowledge and skill they gain in relative power. It is dangerous to the racial position even to employ unskilled Africans in town, for travel and concentration in labour centres diminishes parochialism and develops African nationalism. Any expansion of material scale in the African group threatens the caste system, for, as we have already pointed out (*vide supra*, p. 112), the wider the relative material scale of a group the greater its relative power. Some racialists have indeed been driven to advocate total segregation, and the use of European labour only, in towns,[1] but few are prepared to accept the economic implications of this.

In the scientific field racialism involves not only restriction of further research, but the loss of existing knowledge. Not only must Einstein cease to work in Germany, but his discoveries must be ignored there. If race be the supreme value, the work of those of an alien 'race' cannot be valuable, and the destruction of it is the only logical course. Twenty-five thousand volumes, scientific as well as literary works, were burnt outside the University of Berlin on 13 May 1933. Among them were the writings of Sigmund Freud. To maintain science at its present level involves universal give and take. If communication with all except the members of the chosen race, living and dead, cease, the body of scientific knowledge must shrink. Alexandrine science decayed with the Roman Empire, and the expansion of scale at the Renaissance was both conditioned by, and a condition of, the rediscovery and development of ancient science. In the social field the opposition between racial philosophy and science is even more obvious. Objective study of biology and of sociology must be abandoned, since these sciences contradict the dogma of race. Biologists demonstrate the absurdity of the dogma of 'racial purity', and of the dogma that all Germans are 'Aryan' in race:[2] sociologists show that factors other than race are the main determinants of cultural difference.

The Nazis themselves admit the incompatibility between their dogmas and science: 'The charge of our enmity to science is true... if the complete absence of preconceptions

---

[1] E.g. Professor A. C. Cilliers of Stellenbosch, speaking to the Union of English-speaking South Africans in Cape Town, advocated the transportation of all Union natives to a 'National Home' in Central Africa. Reported *Daily Despatch*, East London, 12 Feb. 1943.

[2] Cf. J. S. Huxley and A. C. Haddon, *We Europeans, passim.*

and predispositions, unrestrained objectivity, are to be taken as characteristic of science. The old idea of science has gone for ever. The new science is entirely different from the idea of knowledge that found its value in an unchecked attempt to reach the truth.'[1] Nevertheless, few racialists realize the implications of their policy in, say, the field of medicine.

Lastly, racialism excludes the ideal of future equality. It makes nonsense of the philosophy that in the distant future 'when they are fit for it' Africans may take their place with the civilized. It involves the abandonment of any ideal of the brotherhood of man and of a current interpretation of Christian doctrine.

Non-racialism involves no colour bar, whether legal or conventional. It involves equal economic and educational opportunities for all races, and it involves freedom to marry between the races. It implies economic expansion—a development of markets through a rising standard of living in the poorer groups—and a corresponding development in science and techniques. The necessary structural form of a non-racial society is subordination in the wider relations combined with autonomy in the narrower, that is, control of international relations and of big business, combined with individual and local autonomy. This form can have no existence apart from a wide religious inclusiveness— a lively concern for the welfare of other nations, other races, other classes.

These are the alternative forms of resolution of the racial opposition in Central Africa. It is an inescapable choice before our society. There is a relative autonomy only in the form and the date of the resolution.

---

[1] The Minister of Science and Education, at the five hundred and fiftieth anniversary of the founding of the University of Heidelberg. Quoted by E. M. Forster in his *Nordic Twilight*, p. 16.

Contractions of scale have occurred—the break up of the Roman Empire is an obvious example. Contraction of scale such as is involved in consistent racialism, restrictionism and nationalism can, however, only result from the most violent disequilibrium, for the relations abandoned have positive value in our present society. A lower standard of living will not be accepted as a permanency, except as the solution of disequilibrium even more violent than now exists. Choice of less or more disequilibrium in our time thus coincides with choice of resolution in a society of greater or less scale.

(d) Conclusion

In conclusion, we want to repeat that the systematic theory of society we have here attempted to construct is scientific, that is, hypothetical. Some axioms we are bound, as scientists, to assume dogmatically. In particular, we are bound to assume that the facts of the social field are objectively intelligible; that, however obscure their relations seem, a system of lucid concepts can be found that will illuminate them. But this is not to assume that the particular system we have found is wholly adequate. That society is a nexus of relations tending inevitably towards equilibrium; that its equilibrium can be disturbed; that in society and in every relation of society there are three material elements, three religious elements and three structural forms; that the most general objective characteristic in which societies differ is their scale; that between the material and religious elements of society there is a relative autonomy; that our present disequilibrium is due to the outrunning in scale of the religious by the material elements of society—these are not articles of faith with us but tentative suggestions based on a limited knowledge of a small area of human society to-day. If anywhere we have seemed to assert these suggestions dogmatically we beg the reader to discount the semblance and to remember

> That nature still defeats
> The frowsty science of the cloistered men,
> Their theory, their conceits; . . . [1]

[1] V. Sackville-West, *The Land*, p. 24.

INDEX